The New Novel in France
Theory and Practice
of the *Nouveau Roman*

Twayne's Critical History of the Novel

Herbert Sussman, Series Editor
Northeastern University

The New Novel in France

Theory and Practice of the *Nouveau Roman*

Arthur E. Babcock
University of Southern California

Twayne Publishers
An Imprint of Simon & Schuster Macmillan
New York

Prentice Hall International
London   Mexico City   New Delhi   Singapore   Sydney   Toronto

Twayne's Critical History of the Novel Series

The New Novel in France: Theory and Practice of the Nouveau Roman
Arthur E. Babcock

Copyright © 1997 by Twayne Publishers
All rights reserved. No part of this book may be reproduced or transmitted in any form or by any means, electronic or mechanical, including photocopying, recording, or by any information storage and retrieval system, without permission in writing from the Publisher.

Twayne Publishers
An Imprint of Simon & Schuster Macmillan
1633 Broadway
New York, NY 10019–6785

Library of Congress Cataloging-in-Publication Data
Babcock, Arthur E.
    The new novel in France: theory and practice of the nouveau roman
/ Arthur E. Babcock
        p.   cm.—(Twayne's critical history of the novel)
    Includes bibliographical references and index.
    ISBN 0–8057–7858–6 (alk. paper)
        1. French fiction—20th century—History and criticism.
    2. Experimental fiction, French—History and criticism.   I.   Title.
    II. Series.
    PQ671.B25   1997
    843'.91409 dc21   96-39135
                                                  CIP

The paper used in this publication meets the minimum requirements of American National Standard for Information Sciences—Permanence of Paper for Printed Library Materials. ANSI Z39.48–1984. ∞™

10 9 8 7 6 5 4 3 2 1

Printed in the United States of America

To my mother and in memory of my father

Contents

Acknowledgments

I am grateful for the support and assistance of my colleagues at the University of Southern California, most particularly Carol Hofmann, Peggy Kamuf, Albert Sonnenfeld, and Peter Starr, who generously shared their expertise with me, and to the university administration for sabbatical and study leaves in support of the writing of this book. My students as well have been a supportive but critical audience for my ideas. Herbert Sussman and Margaret Dornfeld at Twayne showed themselves to be exemplary editors in both judgment and patience.

Chronology

1959   Duras: *Hiroshima mon amour*; Robbe-Grillet: *Dans le labyrinthe*; Sarraute: *Le Planétarium*; *Yale French Studies* special issue on "Midnight Novelists."

1960   Butor: *Degrés, Répertoire*; Duras: *Dix heures et demie du soir en été*; Robbe-Grillet: *L'Année dernière à Marienbad*; Simon: *La Route des Flandres* (receives Prix de L'Express).

1962   Butor: *Mobile*; Duras: *L'Après-midi de M. Andesmas.*

1963   Robbe-Grillet: *Pour un nouveau roman*; Sarraute: *Les Fruits d'or.*

1964   Duras: *Le Ravissement de Lol V. Stein*; Robbe-Grillet's first American lecture tour.

1965   Butor: *6.810.000 Litres d'eau par seconde.*

1967   Butor: *Portrait de l'artiste en jeune singe.*

1968   Sarraute: *Entre la vie et la mort.*

1969   Duras: *Détruire, dit-elle*; Simon: *La Bataille de Pharsale.*

1970   Robbe-Grillet: *Projet pour une révolution à New York*; Simon: *Orion aveugle.*

1971   Simon: *Les Corps conducteurs*; Cerisy colloquium on the New Novel.

1972   Sarraute: *Vous les entendez?*

1973   Simon: *Triptyque*; Cerisy colloquium on Butor.

1974   Duras: *India Song*; Cerisy colloquium on Simon.

1975   Cerisy colloquium on Robbe-Grillet.

1976   Simon: *Leçon de choses.*

1980   Roland Barthes and Jean-Paul Sartre die in Paris.

1981   Robbe-Grillet: *Djinn*; Simon: *Les Georgiques.*

1983   Sarraute: *Enfance.*

1984   Duras: *L'Amant* (receives Prix Goncourt); Robbe-Grillet: *Le Miroir qui revient.*

1985   Simon receives the Nobel prize for literature.

1987   Simon: *L'Invitation.*

1989   Simon: *L'Acacia.*

1991   Duras: *L'Amant de la Chine du Nord.*

1996   Marguerite Duras dies in Paris.

1

Introduction

In 1958, the journal *Esprit* published a special issue on the "nouveau roman."[1] This event is often taken to be the official debut of the New Novel, but not in the sense that *Esprit* was attempting to launch a new literary movement or even to coin the phrase "nouveau roman," which had already occurred in print.[2] Rather, in publishing this volume, the editors of *Esprit* meant only to respond to several requests made at a recent scholarly meeting. Moreover, the center-piece of the issue was not the kind of literary manifesto familiar to those who know the history of French literature but a stocktaking, composed largely of book reviews, culled from the literary press, of a number of contemporary novelists who were producing innova-tive works. The following year, *Yale French Studies* devoted an issue to these same novelists, initiating the American academic commu-nity's interest in the New Novel that would endure throughout its history.[3]

What both these special issues illustrate is the remarkable speed with which the notion of the New Novel captured the interest of a large segment of the intellectual community, in both France and the United States. Although some of the writers who became known as *nouveaux romanciers*, or New Novelists, had begun writing earlier, it was in 1954, when Roland Barthes published his first article on Robbe-Grillet, that people began to speak in terms of a new novelis-tic aesthetic.[4] That two prestigious and influential journals should, only a few years later, devote entire issues to the phenomenon in response to popular demand is evidence of the amount of interest it generated.

The *Yale French Studies* issue was entitled "Midnight Novelists," in recognition of the central role played in the New Novel by Jérôme Lindon's publishing house, Les Editions de Minuit, so called because it had begun as a clandestine publishing operation during the German occupation of France during World War II. Most of the New Novelists were published by this press, even those whose first books were published elsewhere. Not all of them remained with the

press, but the early years of the New Novel are inextricably connected with it. In 1955, Lindon strengthened this connection by
appointing Alain Robbe-Grillet, then as now the most famous of the
New Novelists, to the position of literary consultant.

One reason that interest in the New Novel rose so rapidly is that it
generated from the beginning differences of opinion ranging in
intensity from energetic debate to full-blown polemics. John Sturrock points out that many who popularized the term *"nouveau
roman"* in fact used it pejoratively.[5] New Novels defy readerly
expectations of familiar novelistic technique, often discarding plot,
character, and chronology; some seem to consist primarily of page
after bewildering page of excruciatingly minute descriptions of
mundane objects. Robbe-Grillet, as the most vociferous proponent
of the New Novel, has attracted the liveliest criticism: "boring,"
"unreadable," "sterile," "inhuman," "dogmatic," and even "totali-
tarian" are adjectives that some have used. For his part, Robbe-
Grillet responded to attacks on him with theoretical articles arguing
that the novel as it was understood in 1955 was scandalously over-
due for change. "Obsolete notions" such as character, story, and
commitment (this last is an allusion to the *engagement* of the existentialist writers) should be discarded. Never modest in his choice of
target, he argued that the novel as practiced by Balzac in the 1830s
was an impossibility for writers of the mid twentieth century and
that Robbe-Grillet's immediate predecessors, Sartre and Camus—
then at the height of their careers and influence—produced novels
contradictory to their own philosophies.

None of these assertions was calculated to please the French literary establishment, which held that Robbe-Grillet, trained as an
agronomist, had no understanding of literature:

Of all the remedies devised to save the Novel—from the epistolary novel to
the diary novel, from the documentary to Science Fiction, from interior
monologue to the flashback, yours is certainly the most radical. Reading
your books has the effect that MacMahon identified in typhoid fever: one
either dies from it or emerges feeble-minded. Reflect upon this axiom,
Robbe-Grillet: *each reader that you gain is a reader lost to literature.* Unless Literature is in fact that shapeless, voiceless, paralyzed thing one encounters in
your books. . . .

Burn your books, Robbe-Grillet! Deliver us from that mildew spreading
over our Letters. . . . Save your time and ours. Study the metric system,
since that is your passion![6]

American observers on the whole did not often reach this level of invective; indeed, at some points in the history of the New Novel it appeared to many that these writers received a warmer reception in the United States than in France. There were, however, some notably hostile reactions on this side of the Atlantic. Truman Capote, for example, entitled his 1963 review of Michel Butor's *Mobile* "The $6 Misunderstanding," by which he meant the reader's mistaken belief that six dollars ought to buy a book that can actually be read. Capote used the occasion of this review to get off a few shots against the New Novel as a whole: "The anti-novel novelists (anti-writing writers, really) continue to be the smartest mannequins in the show-rooms of Parisian haute-culture; and, to judge from the latest and cutest displays of Robbe-Grillet *et cie*, it would seem that we must prepare for an even vaguer *nouvelle vague*."[7]

Even serious academic writing often adopted an apocalyptic tone. It seemed to some critics that literature itself was coming to an end, whether they viewed that possibility with alarm or as the long-overdue collapse of a boring and reactionary notion of culture; the latter point of view was well represented among students and professors of literature in the 1960s. Indeed, throughout its history, the New Novel found most of its defenders in university circles, a fact that did not pass unnoticed among its detractors. When the journalist Jean Dutour debated Robbe-Grillet on the popular French television program *Apostrophes* in 1978, he delivered the ultimate withering criticism: "The *professors* are on your side!"[8]

When a debate reaches this level, it has ceased to be enlightening. Some have concluded that there was not much worthwhile substance to the debate, that "New Novel" was at best a term whose only use was inflammatory.[9] Given that the notion of the New Novel revolved around a single publisher and that the chief proponent for the movement was employed by the same publisher, another negative conclusion is that the New Novel was in fact not much more than a publicity campaign.[10]

Indeed, the validity of the term "New Novel" has often been questioned on other grounds as well. The cohesiveness of the group has never been very strong, and the list of who is and who is not considered a New Novelist has evolved a good deal. The *Esprit* issue of 1958 included the following writers: Samuel Beckett, Michel Butor, Jean Cayrol, Marguerite Duras, Jean Lagrolet, Robert Pinget, Alain Robbe-Grillet, Nathalie Sarraute, Claude Simon, and Kateb

Yacine. The *Yale French Studies* of 1959 does not contain an overview article attempting to name every New Novelist; moreover, its field is less sharply delineated than the French journal's (the full title is "Midnight Novelists *and others*"). Nevertheless, one reads on the cover of the Yale periodical the names of all but 2 (Lagrolet and Pinget) of the 10 novelists listed in *Esprit*, plus a few others, such as Françoise Sagan, who are not treated as New Novelists. Of the 10 names cited in 1958, the ones that have figured in virtually every enumeration of New Novelists since then are Butor, Robbe-Grillet, Sarraute, and Simon; Pinget is often mentioned as well. Beckett and Duras tend no longer to be associated with the New Novel although their works continue to attract a great deal of attention. In Beckett's case, the consensus is probably that his work is difficult to assimilate to any other; as for Duras, after a period in which she was widely considered a New Novelist, she tended to remain aloof from the other novelists of the group. Other novelists not mentioned by *Esprit* that one would want to add are Claude Ollier and Claude Mauriac, and from a younger group of writers, not associated with the beginnings of the New Novel but appearing at later stages, one can mention Jean Ricardou, Philippe Sollers, and Monique Wittig.

Thus the question of who is and who isn't a New Novelist has always been rather fluid, and particularly at the height of the debate, the grounds given for the inclusion or exclusion of a particular writer have occasionally been quite flimsy. The New Novel's inconsistencies and contradictions remain a genuine problem. To conclude, however, that the New Novel was nothing more than a figment of critics' imaginations is extreme, and one goal of this study is to demonstrate on what grounds one may say that there was such a thing as the New Novel. There can be no question of treating it as a doctrine or as a literary school—even *movement* seems too strong a term—but the conclusion that a given writer was a New Novelist ought to have more basis than simply that writer's desire, or mere willingness, to be included in the classification.

A complicating factor in determining the validity of the term "New Novel" is critics' custom of discerning two (or more) distinct phases in the development of these writers' work. Different observers use different terms for these phases, but a fairly common schema is to refer to the first phase, during the 1950s and early 1960s, as the "phenomenological" New Novel, whereas the second period, from the late 1960s through the 1970s, is known as the "structuralist" phase sometimes called the "*New* New Novel."[11]

These two approaches to the New Novel will be discussed in detail in the next chapter. They are mentioned here to make the important point that the New Novel had a unique relationship with the different critical theories prevalent in France during the years 1950 to 1980, and most significantly with the *changes* in critical theory. David Carroll puts it well:

Were one to write a history of the New Novel, for instance, this history would not consist only of the explanation of the evolution of this particular form of the novel, or of the chronology of the novels themselves taken on their own terms. For the history of the New Novel is also the history of the various theories used to analyze and explain both the form and sense of the various New Novels—the theories which were applied to the New Novel, helped form it, and, in some sense, were transformed by it.[12]

Every critical age tends to reevaluate in its own terms the literature already evaluated and explained by the preceding age, but the interrelationship that Carroll discusses is altogether more profound and more interesting than that. The evolution of the New Novel was simultaneous with the evolution of the theory used to describe it; the people at work on the one were aware of those working on the other—indeed, in some cases they were the same people—and the influence worked in both directions.

This relationship between theory and the novel is found in both phases. When the New Novel appeared in the mid 1950s, existential phenomenology was very much a current body of thought, and Jean-Paul Sartre and Maurice Merleau-Ponty were influential figures in France and elsewhere. The New Novel appeared to many observers as phenomenological, at least in a general and simplified way: the novel was "about" the problematic relationship of human consciousness with the world. Some novelists, such as Robbe-Grillet, produced remarkable passages of neutral description in which ordinary objects appear devoid of the familiar meanings human beings are accustomed to assigning to them. This kind of description can be taken to represent the so-called phenomenological reduction, in which all presuppositions about the material world are put aside in order better to examine the immediate relationship of the world and consciousness. There were during this phenomenological period some examples of cross-fertilization between theorists and novelists, although such occurrences are much more apparent in the second phase. Claude Simon, for example, was much influenced by Merleau-Ponty, who in turn used examples from Simon's novels in his lectures.

When the body of thought known as structuralism began to be applied to literature in the 1960s, the relationship between theory and the novel deepened, and some of the difficulties in the relationship appeared. For example, under the phenomenological approach, it was possible to conclude, and many did, that the New Novel at bottom was an especially rigorous kind of psychological realism, since it *represented* in the most elemental way the relationship of human consciousness with the world. Since the methods were in many cases new, some called the New Novel a "new realism." A fundamental tenet of structuralism, however, is that literature does not *represent* anything outside of its own internal, constitutive structures. Theories of literary realism, new or old, rest on a referential fallacy and should be discarded. Structuralist readings of New Novels often conclude (on excellent evidence, let it be said) that the novel is "about" itself and the process of writing.

There is nothing inherently more troubling about this critical reappraisal than there is about any other. Nor is it in any way problematic that in the late 1960s and 1970s some New Novelists wrote novels that are rather visibly inspired by structuralist theory. What can be confusing, however, are those occasions when New Novelists or others yield to the impulse to appear consistent at all costs, to reconcile past theoretical statements with current theoretical convictions. It is one thing to argue that a novel once held to be an example of psychological realism is better understood as antireferential metafiction; it is quite another to suppress all evidence that one's theoretical ideas were once different from what they are now, and such a move can only contribute to the feeling that the term "New Novel" does not really mean anything.

Moreover, the advent of structuralism was itself an upheaval considerably larger than the one produced by the New Novel. The structuralist quarrel added another layer of polemics to questions about the New Novel, with more exaggerated claims and dismissive rebuttals. While the New Novel was certainly not the only corpus with which the proponents of structuralism advanced their case, many structuralist analyses of the New Novel had the dual purpose of analyzing a text and making a theoretical point. The New Novel was thus embroiled in a second polemical discussion, with damaging results.

Producing a revolution in the novel and 15 years later contributing to another, different revolution in criticism is a tall order. Claims of being new if issued often enough begin to sound more like claims of fashionability, and by the time structuralism had faded from the scene there was not much interest, though there was some, in proceeding to the New New New Novel. Indeed, not every New Novelist participated in the second phase. Of the writers discussed in this study, only Robbe-Grillet and Simon were enthusiastic participants in the structuralist period. Butor by that time had abandoned the novel for other forms, Sarraute was not really at ease with the arguments advanced during those years, and Duras had ceased to associate herself with the group. Some New Novelists even claimed that the New Novel as a meaningful concept did not survive much past the first phase. When Claude Ollier was asked in a 1983 interview why he spoke of the New Novel only in the past tense, he replied:

As a living thing, the New Novel had already reached the end at the time of the Cerisy colloquium in 1971. Some continued on, but one or two others chose the path of facileness and attempted to monopolize the name. Which means that 20 years later, what is called the New Novel is something completely different. I was pleased at the time when my books were called New Novels! But now, certainly not![13]

Today, with the New Novel almost a half century old, one sometimes hears it dismissed an outdated movement that never lived up to its own promises. There is some justification in such a view, but it is in the nature of any avant garde to make ambitious claims, and one might make the same criticisms of such movements as surrealism, naturalism, even romanticism. Rather than attack the New Novelists as though the polemics of the 1950s and 1960s were still ongoing, it seems more productive to take the position that the time has come for a fair and dispassionate appraisal.

This study proposes, then, to give some of the history of the New Novel and to determine what place it might be assigned in the literature of the twentieth century, now nearly at its end. I have made the choice to consider the New Novel as a cohesive group, to tell the story of a movement (this movement which wasn't one, to paraphrase Luce Irigaray) and not the stories of the individual writers who at one time or another may have been considered New Novelists. To do so, I therefore concentrate on the beginnings of the New Novel, when it was most nearly a cohesive movement, and on the novels written during the 1950s by the core writers: Robbe-Grillet,

Sarraute, Butor, Simon, and Duras. More recent books by these writers will also be discussed, in order both to follow the New Novel through its second phase and to give some idea of what these writers later produced.

Preceding such a discussion, however, is an overview of the theoretical context in which the New Novel was discussed, for theory and practice truly go hand in hand in this case. As already suggested, the theories used to explain the New Novel evolved so much that their development is a story in its own right. Moreover, the first chapter in that story is especially intriguing. The effect of some of the earliest theorizing about the New Novel, by both critics and novelists, was to create a myth of the New Novel that is remarkable for both its capacity to mislead and its longevity.

2

Theory

Many of the New Novelists and some of their advocates have cautioned against an excessive concentration on theory in discussions of the New Novel. Their first objection, reasonable enough, is that to treat the New Novel primarily as a matter of theoretical interest is to overlook that these novels are first creative works of art. Robbe-Grillet, for example, has often said that he set out to write novels, not to formulate theory, and that his subsequent role as a theorist was thrust on him when he discovered to his dismay that in the mind of his critics, his creative work violated the "rules" of novelistic composition. Only then did he attempt to explain himself in theoretical terms. Indeed, Robbe-Grillet's first theoretical writings were a series of articles that the magazine *L'Express* commissioned from him in 1955–56, once the theoretical polemic had already been initiated by others. Moreover, readers who expect each novel to be a statement of theoretical principle are likely to seize on variations of creative practice as theoretical inconsistencies, and thus to attach the wrong importance to them.

The second objection is that to focus exclusively on theory is to invite the misapprehension that the New Novel was a literary school or movement, on the model of, say, surrealism, with Robbe-Grillet in the role of André Breton, surrealism's founder and principal theorist. The temptation is great to assume that, since what one is dealing with is a theory, all New Novelists *have* a theory, and if these theories are not in fact identical, there is at least a great degree of congruence among them. In fact, however, although Robbe-Grillet and Sarraute have each published theoretical books, those two books are quite different, and other New Novelists, such as Claude Simon and Marguerite Duras, have shown little interest in theorizing about their own novelistic practice or about the novel in general.

Nevertheless, the New Novel cannot be discussed at all without considerable attention to theory. The term "New Novel," even if one deliberately defines it in the loosest possible way, remains a theoretical formulation: what distinguishes these novelists from their predecessors is not thematic or philosophical in nature but that they have a concern for the novel as literary form. In the first essay of his theoretical work *Pour un nouveau roman* (*For a New Novel*), entitled "The Use of Theory," Robbe-Grillet tries to avoid giving the impression that he is writing the manifesto of a literary movement:

If in many of the pages that follow, I readily employ the term *New Novel*, it is not to designate a school, nor even a specific and constituted group of writers working in the same direction; the expression is merely a convenient label applicable to all those seeking new forms for the novel, forms capable of expressing (or of creating) new relations between man and the world, to all those who have determined to invent the novel, in other words, to invent man.[1]

Even the rather modest claim that the novel form must evolve, that the traditional nineteenth-century novel is not appropriate to the twentieth-century human situation, rests on so many theoretical considerations that it is quite futile to claim that discussion of theory is inappropriate to study of the New Novel. And, it should be added, Robbe-Grillet himself surely invites attention to theory when he writes, in a book that begins with the protestation that he is not a theorist of the novel, that he expects that the new kind of novel that he and others are beginning to write will culminate in "a revolution more complete than those which in the past produced such movements as romanticism or naturalism," thus likening his enterprise to two of the more self-conscious schools of French literature, complete with leaders, manifestos, and journalistic polemics (*For a New Novel*, 16). So theory there certainly is; what one must do is to avoid the error that theory is all there is and that one theorist's views are applicable to all other practitioners.

The most important theoretical statements produced by the New Novelists are Robbe-Grillet's *For a New Novel* (1963) and Nathalie Sarraute's *L'Ere du soupçon* (*The Age of Suspicion;* 1956). Together, these two books are an excellent introduction to the theoretical issues at stake in the New Novel.

For a New Novel

The beginning of Robbe-Grillet's literary career shows that while he may not have become a theorist by choice, theory quickly became at least associated with him. His first (published) novel, *Les Gommes* (*The Erasers*), was published in 1953 by Les Editions de Minuit, and although it was not successful with the general public it did attract the attention of the soon-to-be-influential critic Roland Barthes. Barthes's early articles on Robbe-Grillet, "Littérature objective" (1954) and "Littérature littérale" (1955), helped to draw attention to Robbe-Grillet, and it is significant that his career was thus linked at the outset with that of the critic who was to exemplify French theory for the next quarter century. His second novel, *Le Voyeur* (*The Voyeur*), published in 1955, had something of a *succès de scandale*, mostly because of the storm of academic protest it generated, and it was then, in 1955–56, that Robbe-Grillet, exasperated by the hostile reaction to his first two books, accepted the invitation of *L'Express* to write a series of articles on the broad topic "Literature Today." Some of these articles will sound familiar to the reader of Robbe-Grillet's later theoretical volume *For a New Novel*: "Why the Death of the Novel," "Socialist Realism Is Bourgeois," and "He Writes Like Stendhal." By the time he wrote "A Future for the Novel" and "Nature, Humanism, Tragedy" in the *Nouvelle revue française* in 1956 and 1958, both of which are reprinted in *For a New Novel*, Robbe-Grillet was well established as a theorist of the novel.

If a single preoccupation can be said to characterize all aspects of Robbe-Grillet's theory of the novel it is that the relationship between human beings and the world has changed since the middle of the nineteenth century, and that critical assumptions about the novel in the 1950s fail to take that fact into account. What is most at stake is the intelligibility of the world; in the traditional novel, every aspect of technique "tended to impose the image of a stable, coherent, continuous, unequivocal, entirely decipherable universe" (*For a New Novel*, 32). Twentieth-century man enjoys no such stability, yet novelists and critics, thinking that technique has no ideological implications and is thus "innocent," continued to regard an outdated conception of the novel as absolute and permanent. Arguing that all attempts in France during the first half of the twentieth century to revitalize the novel produced at most isolated innovative works that did nothing to transform the genre, Robbe-Grillet claims that the prevailing conception of the novel in France in 1955 dates from the early nineteenth century and in some respects even earlier than that. Readers still expect, and critics still admire, novels that resemble those of the nineteenth-century realist Honoré de Balzac or of

Marie-Madeleine de La Fayette, whose *Princesse de Clèves*, published in 1678, is the model for the French psychological novel. Whole passages from these novelists, he complains, could be inserted into many modern novels with only minimal changes and not occasion the slightest surprise on the part of the reader or anything but the warmest praise from critics (p. 16).

Although Robbe-Grillet's rhetoric is often revolutionary, he is fully aware of his predecessors. In some of his more attenuated statements about the "newness" of the New Novel, he argues that all he and his like-minded contemporaries want to do is to continue the development of the genre initiated by such novelists as Flaubert, Dostoevsky, Proust, Kafka, Joyce, and Faulkner, among others (p. 136). These writers belong to what is today called the modernist tradition, and one might expect a revolutionary writer of the 1950s to be what is called today postmodern. But Robbe-Grillet saw himself to be working in a critical climate that had not yet understood the lessons of the modernists, and he was writing against a much earlier tradition, that of Balzac and nineteenth-century realism. This is the tradition that modernism opposed as well, and Robbe-Grillet today is often thought of as a modernist despite his radical stance, which in the context of the 1950s we would normally call postmodernist.[2]

In "A Future for the Novel" and "Nature, Humanism, Tragedy," Robbe-Grillet makes one of his most famous arguments, the one that is associated with one of the most famous (or notorious) aspects of his early novels, the meticulous, "scientific," "objective" description of objects. Most traditional novelistic description, he argues, fails to preserve what is the first and most interesting attribute of things, that they simply *are there*. Traditional novelists never present a thing apart from its meaning: Balzac never describes an empty chair, for example, except to signify that such-and-such a character is absent, and the entire existence of the chair is subordinated to the meaning Balzac overlays on it. Such anthropomorphic metaphors as "majestic mountain" or "pitiless sun" project human meaning into a physical world that exists quite independently without such meaning. At most, literature sets aside the category "absurd" for cases in which an element of the world fails to yield this human signification, but the category is intended only for the occasional frustration of the urge to find meaning everywhere, the "residue," as Robbe-Grillet puts it (p. 19). Moreover, the absurd then becomes in its turn a kind of meaning, as Jonathan Culler explains: "Camus's revolt against literature did not carry very far, for he made the meaninglessness of the world a *theme*; things still had meaning: they signified 'absurdity.' "[3]

What Robbe-Grillet wanted was a novel that would reflect more radically the truth about the world:

> But the world is neither significant nor absurd. It *is*, quite simply. That, in any case, is the most remarkable thing about it. And suddenly the obviousness of this strikes us with irresistible force. All at once the whole splendid construction collapses; opening our eyes unexpectedly, we have experienced, once too often, the shock of this stubborn reality we were pretending to have mastered. Around us, defying the noisy pack of our animistic or protective adjectives, things *are there*. Their surfaces are distinct and smooth, *intact*, neither suspiciously brilliant nor transparent. All our literature has not yet succeeded in eroding their slightest corner, in flattening their slightest curve. (p. 19)

Perhaps the most famous example of Robbe-Grillet's description, because it has been quoted by both his admirers and his detractors, is the following passage from *The Erasers*, which describes a plate of salad in a cafeteria vending machine:

> A quarter of tomato that is quite faultless, cut up by the machine into a perfectly symmetrical fruit.
> The peripheral flesh, compact, homogeneous, and a splendid chemical red, is of an even thickness between a strip of gleaming skin and the hollow where the yellow, graduated seeds appear in a row, kept in place by a thin layer of greenish jelly along a swelling of the heart. This heart, of a slightly grainy, faint pink, begins—toward the inner hollow—with a cluster of white veins, one of which extends toward the seeds—somewhat uncertainly.
> Above, a scarcely perceptible accident has occurred: a corner of the skin, stripped back from the flesh for a fraction of an inch, is slightly raised.[4]

Film, writes Robbe-Grillet, who would shortly become involved in the first of his several cinematic projects, is better suited than literature to this view of the world, for while in the cinema objects and gestures can of course have meaning, the meaning never quite manages to dominate the spectator's attention to the complete exclusion of the material reality of the thing. Indeed, the meaning is somehow something extra, even out of place (p. 20).

Robbe-Grillet's theoretical insistence on description, as well as the dramatically unorthodox descriptions in his novels, inspired the term *école du regard* (the school of the gaze) for his work, and he himself was often called *chosiste* ("thing-oriented" is the somewhat awkward translation). These terms are oversimplifications and even misleading, but it must be said that Robbe-Grillet in a sense invited them by his forceful, sometimes polemical arguments. In the third essay of *For a New Novel*, "Nature, Humanism, Tragedy," he attacks two of the most influential writers of the time, Albert Camus and Jean-Paul Sartre, on the matter of description and its philosophical implications.

Noting that Camus's first novel, *L'Etranger* (*The Stranger*; 1943), is remarkable for its sometimes flat style (Sartre wrote in his review of the book that Camus had rejected anthropomorphism),[5] Robbe-Grillet examines Camus's novelistic practice in light of his celebrated notion of the absurd. For Camus, the absurd arises from the confrontation of man and a world that refuses to yield to human reason.[6] There results a discrepancy, or "divorce," between man and the world. But in Robbe-Grillet's view it is a curious divorce, for despite Camus's supposed rejection of anthropomorphism he still composes such images as the countryside "swollen with sunlight," soil "the color of blood," and sun that has "cast anchor in an ocean of molten metal" (p. 65). These human and humanizing descriptions, says Robbe-Grillet, show that Camus has portrayed not a divorce between man and the world but rather a lover's quarrel, conducted in the hope of reconciliation (p. 64). The absurd, then, is a fundamentally tragic view of the human situation, and tragedy, says Robbe-Grillet, echoing Barthes's argument in "Littérature littérale," is in the last analysis a means of recuperating and justifying human suffering. Camus confronts the strangeness of the world only in terms that reveal a hidden complicity between man and things.

Robbe-Grillet's argument about Sartre's *La Nausée* (*Nausea*; 1938) is more complex, perhaps because early in the novel Sartre appears to foresee, and to reject, the very kind of description that appears in Robbe-Grillet's work. The protagonist of *Nausea*, Antoine Roquentin, is in the grip of a new and unsettling relationship with ordinary objects, which suddenly seem to him to have lost all their familiarity. He begins to keep a diary in order to understand what is happening to him:

The best thing to do would be to write down events from day to day. Keep a diary to see clearly. . . . I must say how I see this table, this street, the people, my packet of tobacco, since *those* are the things which have changed. . . . For instance, here is a cardboard box holding my bottle of ink. I should try to say how I saw it *before* and how I ——— it now. [Roquentin leaves a blank space in place of a word.]

Well, it's a rectangular parallelepiped, it stands out from—that's stupid, there's nothing to say about it.[7]

The descriptive phrase "rectangular parallelepiped," rejected here as "stupid," is not too different from some of Robbe-Grillet's geometrical descriptions, so he goes to some lengths to explain why Sartre's novel implies a view of things that he rejects. Once again, his argument is that what at first looks like a demonstration of the radical strangeness of the world is in reality based on a fatal intimacy between man and objects.

It is significant, Robbe-Grillet argues, that many of Roquentin's confrontations with objects are based on the sense of touch or smell rather than on sight. On this point Robbe-Grillet is perhaps again following Barthes's comments in "Littérature objective," in which he praises Robbe-Grillet's use of the purely visual in *The Erasers*:

Traditional realism accumulates qualities as a function of an implicit judgment: its objects have shapes, but also odors, tactile properties, memories, analogies, in short they swarm with significations; they have a thousand modes of being perceived, and never with impunity, since they involve a human movement of disgust or appetite. Instead of this sensorial syncretism, at once anarchic and oriented, Robbe-Grillet imposes a unique order of apprehension: the sense of sight.[8]

Even when Roquentin's encounter with an object is based on sight, says Robbe-Grillet, it is most often the *color* of the thing rather than its shape that is disturbing. Colors, he argues, are for Roquentin analogous to touch, in that color sensations act on him as both an offer and a withdrawal of intimacy (p. 66). Indeed, Roquentin describes many of his visual relations with things in terms of the other senses. In the crucial scene of the novel, the nausea-producing chestnut tree root is black, but "[i]t *looked* like a colour, but also . . . like a bruise or a secretion, like an oozing—and something else, an odour, for example, it melted into the odour of wet earth, warm, moist wood, into a black odour that spread like varnish over this sensitive wood, in a flavour of chewed, sweet fibre. I did not simply *see* this black."[9]

From these descriptions Robbe-Grillet concludes that this, too, is a tragic universe: what troubles Roquentin about objects is his similarity to them ("I *was* the root"),[10] and what drives him and the book is his redemption. If, on the other hand, one wants to render a non-human universe of things, Roquentin's rejected attempt at a minimalist description of his ink box is the technique that Robbe-Grillet recommends: "To describe things, as a matter of fact, is deliberately to place oneself outside them, confronting them. It is no longer a matter of appropriating to oneself, of projecting anything onto them. Posited, from the start, as *not being man*, they remain constantly out of reach and are, ultimately, neither comprehended in a natural alliance nor recovered by suffering" (p. 70).

One wonders if Robbe-Grillet had Sartre's rectangular parallelepiped in mind when he composed, in *La Jalousie* (*Jealousy*), the following description of the arrangement of trees on a banana plantation: "Furthermore, instead of being rectangular like the one above it, this patch is trapezoidal; for the stream bank that constitutes its lower edge is not perpendicular to its two sides—running up the slope—which are parallel to each other. The row on the right side has no more than thirteen banana trees instead of twenty-three."[11]

Robbe-Grillet's discussion of some aspects of novelistic technique other than description also derives from his conviction that the traditional novel rests on a notion of order and intelligibility that is unjustified in the mid twentieth century. Story, for example, is one of what he calls "obsolete notions." What readers have come to expect from the story is that it have "human truth," that it be faithful to reality—which, in Robbe-Grillet's opinion, is the expectation that the story conform to what the reader already thinks he knows about the world, his preconceived notions of reality.

Character, another "obsolete notion," is likewise a readerly expectation generally expressed in terms that do not really reflect the issues that Robbe-Grillet claims are at stake. To meet conventional expectations, the character must not be "a banal *he*, anonymous and transparent" (p. 27) but must have at least one name, and ideally two—Camus's Meursault, whose first name is never mentioned in *The Stranger*, is in this regard slightly suspect, and Kafka's "K" plainly deficient. He must have a family and a heredity, a profession, and a whole set of socioeconomic information of the kind that constituted a person's identity in Balzac's time but that is less pertinent in Robbe-Grillet's. Finally, a character should have a "character," a personality that is more or less consonant with his actions and that permits the reader to understand him, to judge him, and to react emotionally to him. The whole concern for character is typically anthropocentric, dating as it does to a bourgeois cult of the individual, and Robbe-Grillet claims that Kafka's developments in characterization point the way to the modern novel and to Robbe-Grillet's own enterprise.

Finally, there is the matter of psychology, which is one of the areas in which real controversy arose over Robbe-Grillet's theoretical work. First, his argument: the conventional psychological novel, in the tradition of La Fayette, depends on what Robbe-Grillet calls the "myth of depth": "The writer's traditional role consisted in excavating Nature, in burrowing deeper and deeper to reach some ever more intimate strata, in finally unearthing some fragment of a disconcerting secret. Having descended into the abyss of human passions, he would send to the seemingly tranquil world (the world on the surface) triumphant messages describing the mysteries he had actually touched with his own hands" (p. 24). Again, Robbe-Grillet's objection concerns the matter of intelligibility. It is important to note, in light of the controversy that arose over this matter, that Robbe-Grillet condemns here not so much the "descent" into psychological depths as the subsequent triumphant return to the surface with clear messages of understanding about the mysteries encountered.

Robbe-Grillet's third novel, *Jealousy*, published in 1957, seemed to many of his readers to contradict the author's previous fiction and much of his theory. Part of the difficulty is in the book's psychological interest: the reader is situated from start to finish in the consciousness of a jealous husband through whose eyes scenes appear and reappear, sometimes distorted to the point of hallucination. A second part of the problem is that objects become invested with meaning: the mark left by a centipede squashed against a wall comes to represent the husband's jealousy, appearing to grow in size as his obsession develops. Whereas the method Robbe-Grillet called for in "Nature, Humanism, Tragedy" seemed an exercise in objectivity, *Jealousy* works through extreme subjectivism in that nothing is presented to the reader except through the distorting filter of an obsessional mind.

Robbe-Grillet may actually have deepened the puzzlement felt by some of his readers at these unsuspected developments with the explanations he advanced in "New Novel, New Man," first published in 1961 and one of the last essays included in *For a New Novel*. Here he declares that from the beginning he has never been interested in anything but subjectivity, man and man's place in the world. As for his first books and his subsequent notoriety as a *chosiste*, "Even if many objects are presented and are described with great care [in his early fiction], there is always, and especially, the eye which sees them, the thought which re-examines them, the passion which distorts them. The objects in our novels never have a presence outside human perception, real or imaginary; they are objects comparable to those in our daily lives, as they occupy our minds at every moment" (p. 137). This is a pretty fair description of what goes on in *Jealousy*, in which objects are presented through the consciousness of the main character, but these remarks on objects and perception surely clash with the spirit of his earlier distaste for anthropomorphism, as expressed when Robbe-Grillet writes, "[T]here exists something in the world which is not man, which makes no sign to him, which has nothing in common with him" (p. 52).

Critics have disagreed as to whether these objective and subjective aspects of Robbe-Grillet's theory contradict each other, and their lively debate on this question dominated much of the critical discussion of Robbe-Grillet in the 1960s. Some, such as Barthes and Stephen Heath, go so far as to postulate multiple Robbe-Grillets, the nonanthropocentric, *chosiste* author of *The Erasers* and *The Voyeur*, and a second, subjective or even humanist author seen in *Jealousy* and in the film scenario *L'Année dernière à Marienbad* (*Last Year at Marienbad*).[12] Other critics who shared the view that there is a contradiction in Robbe-Grillet's thinking were less circumspect in their judgments, and concluded simply that Robbe-Grillet's theoretical statements are confused.[13]

Still others, notably Bruce Morrissette, have attempted to resolve the contradiction. So far as the newly signifying objects of Robbe-Grillet's writing are concerned, for example, Morrissette points out that even in the essays that established him as *chosiste*, Robbe-Grillet allows for a certain *kind* of meaning that is temporarily associated with objects but located in the human mind, not in any essence or meaning belonging properly to the object itself.[14] In the following passage, written in 1956 and thus before the controversy, Robbe-

Grillet qualifies his *chosiste* argument in a way that seems to allow for his practice in *Jealousy*: "No longer will objects be merely the vague reflection of the hero's vague soul, the image of his torments, the shadow of his desires. Or rather, if objects still afford a momentary prop to human passions, they will do so only provisionally, and will accept the tyranny of significations only in appearance—derisively, one might say—the better to show how alien they remain to man" (*For a New Novel*, 21–22). Morrissette calls this kind of "momentary prop" an "objective correlative," whose meaning is transitory, as opposed to a symbol, whose meaning is neither transitory nor arbitrary, and whose use would really be antithetical to Robbe-Grillet's theory.[15] The view that sustains Robbe-Grillet's theory and his novels is by and large coherent, according to Morrissette, and he identifies this view as existential phenomenology.

This interpretation is at first glance an attractive resolution of the apparent contradiction in Robbe-Grillet's theoretical writings. From this point of view, one could argue that like the existentialists, Robbe-Grillet rejects the world of *essences*, where the meaning of a thing is one of its permanent attributes, for the world of *existence*. Stephen Heath, however, in an exhaustive and authoritative refutation of this argument, points out that there is more to phenomenology than that.[16]

Existential phenomenology, rather than putting man and the world in separate compartments, as Robbe-Grillet seems to want to do, makes them depend on one another in the most profound way. Consciousness, for Sartre, is consciousness *of* something; man becomes aware of himself in the world through his relation to it. As Merleau-Ponty puts it, "[M]an is in the world, and only in the world does he know himself."[17] Thus phenomenology rejects a dualistic view of man and the world. It makes no sense to talk of one without the other; each is in a sense a function of the other, or rather a function of the relation between the two. Robbe-Grillet's earnest wish to expel man and human meaning from the world of things is, for Sartre, nonsensical: "Remove Man, and things are neither nearer nor further away; they no longer *are*."[18]

Thus Roquentin's unsettled feeling in *Nausea* arises from his growing awareness that the meanings, even the definitions, of things are not permanent attributes but rather human inventions. He would prefer to think that meanings and definitions are housed in some platonic region that does not depend on human intervention, and that his life takes place in a stable world of unchanging being. His nausea compels him to realize, however, that the only meanings we find in the world are the ones that we ourselves put there. This realization is troubling to him because meanings that are of purely human origin seem arbitrary and transitory, and because without our projection of meaning into the world, existence is totally formless and quite literally unspeakable. Even the simplest language used by human beings to talk about the world is a projection of meaning; without such projection of meaning, there can be only undifferentiated, senseless existence.

There is thus no way to expunge all human signification from the physical world, for there would then be no way even to discuss that world. That is why Roquentin rejects "rectangular parallelepiped" as a description of the box containing his ink bottle: he had sought one thing he could say about the object with certainty, something that would be an attribute of the box as it truly *is* rather than his projection, and realizes that "rectangular parallelepiped" is as much a human-imposed meaning, a flight of fancy, as the most flowery descriptive language.

In his earlier essays, Robbe-Grillet clearly conceives of a descriptive relation between man and thing from which any possible complicity or intimacy has been expunged. But in existential phenomenology, according to Merleau-Ponty, even the barest kind of geometrical description is necessarily marked by the human meaning that Robbe-Grillet expects it to avoid: "When I say that an object is *on* a table, I always situate myself in my thought as being in the table or in the object and I apply to them a category which in principle corresponds to the relation of my body to external objects. Without this anthropological contribution the word 'on' cannot be distinguished from 'beneath' or 'next to.' "[19] There is, then, no hope for the chaste relation with things that Robbe-Grillet wants; one cannot look at things "without indulgence," as he proposes (*For a New Novel*, 52). There are no doubt degrees of indulgence, and understanding phenomenology does not mean that one must engage in effusion about majestic mountains and the like, but expelling human meaning from the world of things is an ontological impossibility.

So it is not possible to argue that Robbe-Grillet's theoretical ideas about anthropomorphism and description are consistent with existential phenomenology. Since he did not claim that they were, there is as yet no contradiction. The problem is that his *novels*, as opposed to his theoretical essays, seem to support a phenomenological reading, at least in a general way. It is productive to approach *Jealousy*, for example, with phenomenology in mind, and even his earlier novels, such as *Les Gommes*, seem to be more about a *problem* of meaning than about its *elimination*. Robbe-Grillet's theory of description does not describe his novels very well, except for such isolated passages as the cafeteria tomato.

Many of Robbe-Grillet's novels deal with situations that invite the characters to engage in interpretation: a police investigation, a jealous husband whose wife may or may not be sleeping with their neighbor. Such situations readily dramatize and make problematical the human pursuit of meaning in a material world in which meaning is not guaranteed by some transcendent agency but is fluid and changing. The question of the human meaning of objects is absolutely central: a jealous husband does not live in a world full of meaningless objects; he lives with objects (letters, for example) that mean a great deal to him, rightly or not. Robbe-Grillet's first published novel, *Les Gommes*, is the story of a criminal investigation. What makes police work a fruitful model for Robbe-Grillet is the nature of the enterprise: all that detectives have to go on is the physical evidence. Their work is to attempt to reconstruct the crime, to account for the evidence in a meaningful interpretation. But as the evidence accumulates and the witnesses perhaps contradict one another, the detectives' interpretation may seem increasingly flimsy, the product solely of their imagination and desire to solve the crime. Seen this way, there seems to be no contradiction between even Robbe-Grillet's earliest novels and his later claim always to have been interested in subjectivity. The problem is rather in reconciling his theoretical statements about the need to purge the novelistic world of human meaning. Attempting to solve the problem by saying that there was a succession of several different Robbe-Grillets is not particularly helpful, for it is not that he changed over time but that much of his theory is at variance with his practice.

In Robbe-Grillet's own estimation, the problem lies not so much in a second, subjective phase of his thought that so many observers found troubling as in the misimpression certain critics had of the first, objective phase. In agreeing with Morrissette that Barthes's early essays on his work created the myth of a Robbe-Grillet who was "thing-oriented" and "inhuman," Robbe-Grillet in effect blamed much of the apparent contradiction on Barthes: "Barthes has led to a

real distortion of my work."[20] There is some truth in this, in that
Barthes's early essays on Robbe-Grillet tend to isolate particular
aspects of his writing and to disregard others, but it must be said
that Robbe-Grillet is at least as responsible as Barthes for any "distortion": the first essays in *For a New Novel* also vastly overstate the
matter of nonanthropomorphic description and give quite an inac-
curate impression of his novels.

Indeed, the interplay between Robbe-Grillet and his critics is
striking. Robbe-Grillet is always very aware of what is being written
about him, and the impression is inescapable that his theoretical discussions of his own work vary somewhat according to the critical
climate. A specific example of this interplay between Robbe-Grillet
and his critics occurred after the publication of *Jealousy*. The book
first appeared with a jacket blurb written by Robbe-Grillet but
signed "The Editors," who explained that "The narrator of this book
[is] a husband keeping watch on his wife."[21] The writer Maurice
Blanchot, thinking that the publisher had misunderstood the complexities of the book, wrote a strong letter of protest, arguing, and
with considerable justification, that there is no narrator in *Jealousy*,
only a "pure anonymous presence." Even though other commentators admitted that without the hint from Robbe-Grillet they would
have been hopelessly lost in the novel, future editions of the book
appeared without the explanatory notice, in conformity with the
wishes of a distinguished critic if not with the original intention of
the author.

The critical debate over the *chosiste* versus the subjective Robbe-
Grillet did not last much beyond 1970 and ended less with victory
for one side than with a general unspoken agreement to move on to
other questions. It is remarkable, though, that despite critical arguments and Robbe-Grillet's numerous written and spoken protesta-
tions, and despite the subjective aspect of his novels, the myth of the
"thing-oriented" Robbe-Grillet survives to this day. An encyclope-
dia of literary history published in 1994 states, disregarding not only
the evidence of *Jealousy* but of everything else written by Robbe-
Grillet since 1956, that Robbe-Grillet "concentrates on external reality, believing this to be the only one."[22] A 1995 review note in the *Los
Angeles Times* on the English translation of *La Belle captive* states that
Robbe-Grillet's novels "confin[e] themselves to the surfaces of life
that Robbe-Grillet thinks are the only realm credibly investigated by
language."[23] Moreover, one often encounters in the press similar

assertions about the primacy of things and surfaces in the works of *every* New Novelist, including those of Nathalie Sarraute, who held precisely the opposite view. In all likelihood, the *chosiste* myth will persist for as long as anyone remembers the New Novel at all.

The second, or structuralist, phase of the New Novel in the late 1960s and 1970s renewed the controversy surrounding Robbe-Grillet in particular and the New Novel in general. It also introduced new voices into the controversy. Perhaps most notable among these is Jean Ricardou, the leading theorist of this second phase of the New Novel and a novelist himself (*La Prise de Constantinople;* 1965). Ricardou was a vigorous participant in the various colloquia on the New Novel and its practitioners held at Cerisy-la-Salle in the early 1970s. It was at one of these that the term *nouveau nouveau roman* ("New New Novel") was coined.

In general, structuralist theorizing about the New Novel followed the model of Ferdinand de Saussure's linguistics, which held that language is a *relational* system, composed of signs whose value is determined by their relation to other signs in the system rather than by some intrinsic value. Thus, "[I]n language there are only differences *without positive terms*. Whether we take the signified or the signifier, language has neither ideas nor sounds that existed before the linguistic system, but only conceptual and phonic differences that have issued from the system."[24] The structuralist view of literature, then, is of a self-contained system functioning according to its internal laws rather than according to the extraliterary phenomena to which it is naively thought to refer. Thus structuralist discussions of the New Novel take place in the context of a general attack on the notions of referentiality and representation in literature.

Such a view of literature is a dramatic departure from many of the assumptions underlying earlier discussion of the New Novel, including much of *For a New Novel*. Robbe-Grillet's main argument, that an evolving relationship of human beings with their world requires a corresponding evolution of literary practices, is basically referential: literature follows and describes some extraliterary reality, namely, human beings' relationship with the world. Nevertheless, Robbe-Grillet welcomed the new approach to his novels, although adjusting to the new, antireferential understanding of literature led to a few awkward moments. At the 1975 Cerisy colloquium devoted to Robbe-Grillet's work, Ricardou took the novelist to task for arguing, in *For a New Novel*, that anthropomorphic metaphors should not be used by modern writers. If literature is not referential, after all, feelings about the suitability of literary language to the human situation in the real world are irrelevant, and Robbe-Grillet was wrong to want to interfere with the free play of literary structures. Robbe-Grillet's attempt to accommodate himself to this new line of reasoning is somewhat lame: "From the time when I forbade the use of metaphors in general (at the time of *Jealousy*), what interested me was precisely using metaphors, which is seen in my work beginning with *Dans le labyrinthe* (*In the Labyrinth*)."[25]

On the other hand, the new structuralist approach to the New Novel did recognize elements of New Novel theory and practice that had not been well understood before. For example, the reflexive, or metafictional, mechanisms by which a novel takes itself as its own subject interested Robbe-Grillet from the beginning of his career, and if much of *For a New Novel* addresses somewhat different issues, he argues earlier in those pages that the modern novel no longer aims at giving the illusion of reality: "What constitutes the novelist's strength is precisely that he invents, that he invents quite freely, without a model. The remarkable thing about modern fiction is that it asserts this characteristic quite deliberately, to such a degree that invention and imagination become, at the limit, the very subject of the book" (p. 32).

Robbe-Grillet's novels abound in interior duplications of themselves, often representing by analogy the difficulty the reader encounters in extracting meaning from them. The following passage concerns a song sung by one of the plantation workers in *Jealousy* but is applicable as well to the novel itself, with the reader in the role of the "western listener":

The singing is at moments so little like what is ordinarily called a song, a complaint, a refrain, that the western listener is justified in wondering if something quite different is involved. The sounds, despite quite apparent repetitions, do not seem related by any musical law. There is no tune, really, no melody, no rhythm. It is as if the man were content to utter unconnected fragments as an accompaniment to his work.[26]

Structuralist criticism of the second phase added a great deal to the understanding of the New Novel and, in its best moments, profoundly and permanently changed how many of these novels are read. However, it also marked the beginning of the end of "New

Novel" as a valid concept. First, different novelists reacted to the new impetus from Ricardou and others in different ways. If Robbe-Grillet and Simon welcomed the new approach to their novels, Sarraute on the other hand seemed uncomfortable with the implications of the new theories, so whatever cohesion among New Novelists there may have been at first weakened.

Moreover, the application of literary structuralism to questions of the New Novel led to polemics in not only the aesthetic but also the political domain. The formulation of structuralist ideas about the New New Novel coincided with the political upheaval of May 1968 and its aftermath. While many structuralist analyses of the New Novel had no overt political content, Ricardou's discussions were very often aggressively ideological. He objected to any representational function of the literary text not only on aesthetic grounds but because any allusion to literary realism or referentiality was an implicit endorsement of a "ruling ideology" against which the New Novel ought to revolt:

In short, the principle of Terrorism is precisely that of the current ruling ideology, firmly in place since the nineteenth century, with its romantic aspect (in which the essential thing concerns above all the self, and in which the activity of language, of secondary importance, is called Expression) and its realist aspect (in which the essential thing concerns the world, and in which the activity of language, of secondary importance, is called Representation).[27]

This "ruling ideology" was never defined, except to say that Ricardou and the New Novel as he understood it were outside it. Exchanging such highly questionable ideas in a polemical atmosphere does not make for lasting contributions to a discussion, and Ricardou's notion of the New New Novel did not permanently change the terms in which these works are discussed.

A number of years after he published *For a New Novel*, Robbe-Grillet declared that one could suppress all his theoretical writings without changing anything about his novels, but the remark is not to be taken as a rejection of theory, for he went on to say that the theoretical side of his work is contained in the novels themselves.[28] Contradictory or not, even confused, perhaps, Robbe-Grillet's theory remains one of the most compelling and controversial aspects of his work.

The Age of Suspicion

The reader with some experience of Robbe-Grillet's theoretical ideas who comes upon the work of Nathalie Sarraute might very well be excused for thinking not only that the New Novel does not have the cohesiveness of a school but that it is composed of writers so different that the term can have no meaning at all. Whereas Robbe-Grillet wanted the novel to deal with surfaces at the expense of what he calls the "myth of depth," Sarraute's work is concerned almost exclusively with the inner psychological dramas that transpire beneath the surface of a person's external, public life. Certainly Robbe-Grillet showed in *Jealousy* that he could be interested in a kind of psychological novel, and it has been argued here that his *chosiste* reputation is an exaggeration, so the opposition between the two is not complete on this point, but in their theoretical texts Robbe-Grillet and Sarraute have very different ways of talking about the art of the novel.

In her discussion of the kind of novel she advocates, Sarraute uses a vocabulary of interiority and images of the depth that Robbe-Grillet rejects. The things that interest her are to be found "beneath" or "behind" surface behavior; she speaks of "secret recesses," the "subterranean," and Dostoevsky's "underground." The following passage, in which she talks about the effect that certain techniques are intended to produce on the reader, exemplifies this stress on interiority: "Suddenly the reader is on the inside, exactly where the author is, at a depth where nothing remains of the convenient landmarks with which he constructs the characters. He is immersed and held under the surface until the end, in a substance as anonymous as blood, a magma without name or contours."[29] The passage is lyrical, with Sarraute pursuing ever more fundamental images of depth: blood, of course, is what is found inside the body; magma may perhaps be considered even deeper, more primordial, being found beneath the crust of the earth itself. Conversely, she speaks of surfaces in disparaging terms. Writing of novels that enjoy a transitory burst of popularity because of what they seem to tell readers about certain external details of their lives, she explains why such works do not attain lasting admiration: "[W]hat [these works] described was not reality. Or rather, . . . it was only a surface reality, nothing but the flattest, most commonplace sort of semblance" (pp. 129–30). When one contrasts this attitude with, for example, the half page that Robbe-Grillet devotes to a slice of tomato, the conclusion is irresistible that one is dealing with two very different ways of thinking.

Sarraute's remarks on the cinema are another example of her differences with Robbe-Grillet. Both see film as an art that is inherently suited to portraying exteriors. But while Robbe-Grillet considers film a model that the novel should emulate, Sarraute argues that the novel should not try to rival film in an area in which film will always be superior. Here and in her comments on another genre, the theater, Sarraute contends that the novel has its own specific uses and resources. Like film, theater should not tempt novelists to abandon their own ground; she sees the increasing reliance of the modern novel on dialogue as a dangerous trend. First, one should remember that theater attains its effects not just with the printed script but with actors and their interpretation: one cannot expect to succeed if one tries to accomplish the same thing with the novel. Second, the novel should be novelistic rather than give up what makes it unique, which is first and foremost its ability to get *inside* (pp. 106–7). Thus Sarraute's very definition of the novel, her notion of what is "novelistic," is quite different from Robbe-Grillet's.

Given these differences, it is inevitable that Sarraute and Robbe-Grillet should read certain texts in very different ways. Sarraute gives her view of the present state of the novel in the first essay in *The Age of Suspicion*, entitled "From Dostoievski to Kafka" and first published in 1947 in Sartre's *Les Temps modernes*. Her discussion of *The Stranger* in this essay is remarkably parallel to Robbe-Grillet's, except that the terms of value are reversed. Analyzing precisely the same type of image that Robbe-Grillet criticized as anthropomorphic, such as "a drowsy headland" or "an odor of night and flowers," Sarraute speaks approvingly of the character Meursault's "exceptional sensitivity," his "unerring taste," and his "tenderness of a poet" (pp. 21–23). The book then becomes for Sarraute a demonstration that even the so-called *homo absurdus* of existential fiction has, beneath all the external bleakness, emotional responses to the absurd.

Her treatment of Kafka is somewhat similar and leads her to a rather arresting statement of her preferences in fiction. In "From Dostoievski to Kafka," Sarraute identifies two fundamental tendencies in the novel of the end of the nineteenth century and the first half of the twentieth: Dostoevsky's "psychological" approach, and the "situational" novel represented by Kafka (p. 11). She argues that it is the latter that has come to dominate, according to received opinion, what with the existential novel of Sartre and Camus and French admiration for the impersonal, nonintrusive narration of the twentieth-century American novel, a narrative technique known in France as "behaviorist." In the first part of the essay, she establishes that Dostoevsky's characters are all motivated by what Katherine Mansfield called "this terrible desire to establish contact" (p. 33). The psychological drama of this need is played out, as it is in Sarraute's novels, beneath the surface exchanges of human relations. Turning to Kafka, Sarraute at first shows, as she did in the case of Camus, that even in Kafka's world of alienation and radical strangeness, the characters—Joseph K. and Leni in *The Trial*, for example—share this need for contact. However, it is on a much more limited scale; whereas Dostoevsky's characters seek "a total and ever possible fusion of souls," Kafka's characters cannot aim so high. At most, they can hope to become "in the eyes of these people who regard them with such distrust ... not their friend, perhaps, but in any case, their fellow citizen" (pp. 41–42). To justify oneself before anonymous, unapproachable accusers is the vestigial hope of contact left to Kafka's characters, and as it turns out, even that is denied them. Kafka, then, more than Camus, actually portrays a dehumanized universe. In the remarkable conclusion to her essay, Sarraute makes Kafka's nightmare world a chillingly accurate prophecy of the Holocaust (before going off to his death, for example, Joseph K. folds his clothes carefully together) and concludes that Kafka represents a culmination of the purely situational tendency beyond which no one should care to go: "To remain at the point where he left off, or to attempt to go on from there, are equally impossible. Those who live in a world of human beings can only retrace their steps" (p. 50).

The recommendation to "retrace [one's] steps" ("turn back" might be a better translation of the French) is perhaps a curious suggestion from someone who is associated with the *New* Novel. What Sarraute's phrase shows is that she is very conscious of her predecessors and that her relationship with them is of a slightly different order than that claimed by Robbe-Grillet. The predecessors mentioned by Sarraute are, with a few differences, the same modernist novelists cited by Robbe-Grillet: Flaubert, Dostoevsky, Proust, Joyce,

Kafka, and Faulkner. The differences are that Sarraute attaches less importance to the American behaviorist novelists than does Robbe-Grillet for reasons already mentioned, and correspondingly more importance to the psychological novelists of that tradition: Dosto-evsky, Proust, and Woolf.

Sarraute's conception of psychology dates from her first work, *Tropismes* (*Tropisms*), completed in 1937 and published in 1939. The notion of "tropism," by her own account, is also the basis for all her subsequent creative works. The term designates emotional stirrings that transpire beneath the surface of people's speech, actions, even the emotions for which we have conventional names:[30]

These movements, of which we are hardly cognizant, slip through us on the frontiers of consciousness in the form of undefinable, extremely rapid sensations. They hide behind our gestures, beneath the words we speak, the feelings we manifest, are aware of experiencing, and able to define. They seemed, and still seem to me to constitute the secret source of our existence, in what might be called its nascent state.[31]

Tropisms is composed of 18 sketches (6 more were added when the book was reissued by Les Editions de Minuit in 1957) populated by unnamed characters and relatively unstructured by traditional plot. These vignettes, which resemble James Joyce's epiphanies and which may also remind one of Virginia Woolf's sketches,[32] show the emotional complexities that can underlie the most commonplace occurrences and situations. In section VIII, for example, an elderly man takes a grandchild for a walk, taking care to teach the child that one must look both ways before crossing a street. Perhaps by association, he goes from the dangers of traffic to a short discussion of death, telling the child of a time when the grandfather, too, was young. Beneath this apparently benign relationship, however, lies the grandfather's need to dominate the young: "[H]e felt an aching, irresistible need to manipulate them with his uneasy fingers, to bring them as close as possible, to appropriate them for himself" (p. 20). At the end of the section, Sarraute evokes the emotional content of the scene in a highly imaged passage:

The air was still and gray, odorless, and the houses rose up on either side of the street, the flat masses of the houses, closed and dreary, surrounded them as they proceeded slowly along the pavement, hand in hand. And the child felt that something was weighing upon him, benumbing him. A soft choking mass that somebody relentlessly made him take, by exerting upon him a gentle, firm pressure, by pinching his nose a bit to make him swallow it, without his being able to resist—penetrated him, while he trotted docilely along, like a good little boy, nodding his head very reasonably, while it was explained to him that he should always proceed cautiously and look well, first to the right, then to the left, and be careful, very careful, for fear of an accident, when crossing between the lines. (*Tropisms*, 21–22)

The means by which Sarraute intends to convey these tropisms to the reader is important, for if they lie beneath easily definable emotional states, one cannot simply name them. The point of the section cited above is not the narrator's assertion that the grandfather seeks to manipulate, nor is Sarraute's intent at the end to present the scene from the child's point of view:

And since, while we are performing them, no words express them, not even those of the interior monologue—for they develop and pass through us very rapidly in the form of frequently very sharp, brief sensations, without our perceiving what they are—it was not possible to communicate them to the reader otherwise than by means of equivalent images that would make him experience analogous sensations. (pp. vi–vii)

Whereas Proust showed a kindred interest in "an immense profusion of sensations, images, sentiments, memories, impulses, little larval actions that no inner language can convey" (p. 91), his method was traditional psychological analysis. Sarraute's objection to this method is much the same as Robbe-Grillet's: it attempts not to preserve the reality of the emotions but to name them, to bring them into the sphere of rationality where they can be explained and understood: "[Proust] considered them as a sequence of causes and effects which he sought to explain. He rarely—not to say never—tried to relive them and make them relive for the reader in the present, while they were forming and developing, like so many tiny dramas, each one of which has its adventures, its mystery and its unforeseeable ending" (pp. 92–93).

The tropistic drama taking place beneath surface conversation is what Sarraute calls the world of "sub-conversation." Again, Proust is attuned to these hidden meanings, but so interested in them, perhaps, that he seldom leaves it up to the reader to sense what is transpiring: "Should there be the slightest discrepancy between the conversation and the sub-conversation, should they not entirely cover each other, he immediately intervenes; at times, before the character speaks, at others, as soon as he has spoken, to show all he sees, explain all he knows" (p. 108). In contrast, the ideal would be

a technique that might succeed in plunging the reader into the stream of these subterranean dramas of which Proust only had time to obtain a rapid aerial view. . . . This technique would give the reader the illusion of repeating these actions himself, in a more clearly aware, more orderly, distinct and forceful manner than he can do in life, without losing that element of indetermination, of opacity and mystery that one's own actions always have for one who lives them. (pp. 110–11)

These remarks on traditional psychological analysis are just one example of the considerable role that novelistic convention plays in Sarraute's theory. Her objection to traditional methods is principally that they are traditional, that they have become conventions to which the reader has learned to make a set of conventional responses. Traditional psychological analysis, rather than revealing psychological reality, has the paradoxical effect of concealing it, since the reader reacts to it in conventionalized, superficial ways. Balzac's contemporaries did not, of course, find Balzac's technique familiar and traditional: they had to work at it, and in the very difficulty of what was then a new way of communicating lay its power. The same technique used today is an incitement to laziness and a crutch for the unimaginative (p. 60).

This attention to the harmful effects of convention is also behind much of Sarraute's thinking about character, which is the main subject of the essay "The Age of Suspicion." The "suspicion" is felt not only by the reader, grown weary of the endless procession of "unforgettable" characters created by "real novelists" since the time of Balzac, but also by the novelist, who knows the effect on the reader of the traditional character. The fuller the characterization— the more "unforgettable" the character—the more likely the reader is to see in the character one of the literary types made familiar by the long list of "real novelists" the reader has absorbed. The reader will have gained only in breadth, by adding another character to his collection, so to speak, but not in depth, since the reader's very familiarity with the literary type will distract attention from "psychological reality": "And since what the characters gain in the way of facile vitality and plausibility is balanced by a loss of fundamental truth in the psychological states for which they serve as props, he must be kept from allowing his attention to wander or to be absorbed by the characters" (pp. 68–69). This is how one should view the minimalist approach to character in the modern novel, according to Sarraute. One deprives the reader of the usual trappings of character, such as physical description, possessions, social position, name, "personality," in order not to situate the character in too familiar a world.

The concept is very like Robbe-Grillet's notion of the character; Blanchot's description of Robbe-Grillet's characters as "pure anonymous presence" would not be out of place in Sarraute's discussion. Indeed, the discussion of character is probably the closest that Sarraute and Robbe-Grillet come to advocating the same technique: the two passages in which each argues against the traditional "trappings" of the character are very similar. But the real congruence between these two writers is less in the specific techniques they recommend—even when they sound the same theoretically they end up producing very different results—but in their understanding of the importance of convention and familiarity in the novel.

Even here one could argue that their motivations are not exactly the same. Sarraute considers the reader's familiarity with traditional technique to be, finally, an obstacle to the novelist's communication with the reader: "psychological reality" will be masked by conventional categories of thought established by scores of traditional novels. Robbe-Grillet is equally opposed to giving the reader a comfortably familiar world, not so much because familiarity is bad technique but because it is itself a falsification of the real place of man in the universe. Unfamiliarity itself is the "truth" that he wishes to communicate: the feelings of a reader confronted with an unfamiliar novel most closely approximate the phenomenological truth of man's experience in the world. The difference is perhaps a subtle one, and may be due simply to Robbe-Grillet's tendency to give an ideological, rather than purely aesthetic, basis to his arguments. It is for Robbe-Grillet inappropriate to create Balzacian characters in the mid twentieth century not only because the technique has become conventionalized and stale but because one no longer believes in the bourgeois cult of the individual. This kind of argument is not entirely absent from Sarraute's theoretical developments, but her deepest motivations are aesthetic rather than ideological.

Speaking in 1982, long after the cohesiveness of the *nouveau roman* group had ceased to be a pressing issue, Sarraute spoke of her positive feelings for the New Novel without attempting to overstate the similarities among the various writers:

> There has been, however, considerable diversity among us since the beginning. As has already been said, what Alain Robbe-Grillet writes and what I write are exactly the same, except different. In my work, it is a stream of internal movements, and in his, it is an interplay of external stills.
>
> But as far as the freedom of novelistic forms is concerned and the necessity of constantly transforming them in order to keep them alive, we were in agreement. It was a pleasure for me to meet writers much younger than I who shared my opinions.[33]

If one attempts to find agreement between Sarraute's and Robbe-Grillet's theoretical ideas as they are expressed in *The Age of Suspicion* and *For a New Novel*, only a broad statement such as this one by Sarraute is possible, for the two authors take quite different approaches in their theoretical works. In their novelistic *practice*, however, it may well be possible to find a greater degree of congruence.

3

Alain Robbe-Grillet

Robbe-Grillet is not a writer who labored in obscurity for years before being discovered by the literary community; his career made a comparatively rapid start, with *The Erasers, The Voyeur, Jealousy,* and *In the Labyrinth,* all published before 1960, and even today one continues to find fresh critical discussion of his novels of the 1950s. Those years were marked by polemics that no doubt generated more heat than light, but it was also then that serious commentators began to separate critical analysis from journalistic debate; some of the most influential criticism of Robbe-Grillet was written about his early work.

For this reason, it is useful to introduce Robbe-Grillet by foregrounding two of his early novels, *The Erasers* and *Jealousy,* with a look at *Le Rendez-vous/Djinn,* a sample of his later work. Moreover, *The Erasers* and *Jealousy* most usefully support the discussion of *For a New Novel* in the last chapter. Regrettably, Robbe-Grillet's cinema is outside the scope of this study.

The Erasers (1953)

It is something of a commonplace to link the early careers of Robbe-Grillet and Roland Barthes.[1] Their association was of mutual interest and benefit: if Barthes's early articles gave Robbe-Grillet an exposure he would not have had otherwise, Robbe-Grillet's work responded to Barthes's growing theoretical convictions about the nature of writing. Jonathan Culler observes:

At the same time that he was "set on fire" by Brecht, Barthes became a fervent supporter of novelist Alain Robbe-Grillet, to whom four of the pieces in *Essais critiques* are devoted. "What has fascinated me all my life," Barthes affirms, "is the way mankind makes its world intelligible." Robbe-Grillet's novels explore this process by attempting a heroic but impossible elimination of meaning, thus bringing to our attention the ways we are accustomed to make things intelligible.[2]

Perhaps it was this very mutuality that produced a degree of antagonism in their relationship as well; as was shown in the last chapter, each party eventually had to revise its first estimation of the other: Barthes decided there were two Robbe-Grillets, only one of whom responded to Barthes's interests, and Robbe-Grillet blamed Barthes for a "distortion" of his work. Further, in the history of the New Novel, Barthes's readings of Robbe-Grillet led to the first serious critical disagreement (as opposed to journalistic polemics) over the import of these innovative works.

Reading *The Erasers* after gaining some familiarity with Barthes's essay "Objective Literature," as many readers doubtless have, is something of a shock.[3] Led by Barthes's article (and by *For a New Novel*) to expect a radical assault on literary meaning, the reader discovers a text that is remarkably readable, more so than many of Robbe-Grillet's later works. Whereas the reader might expect from all the discussion of nonanthropomorphic description a collection of passages like that describing the slice of tomato, he or she quickly discovers that the novel also possesses a plot, of all things, and a rather intriguing one at that.

The story concerns the detective Wallas, sent by his superiors to a northern European city to investigate what they think is the latest in a series of political murders, all committed at seven-thirty in the evening. What the reader knows but Wallas does not is that the supposed victim, Daniel Dupont, has been only slightly wounded, has taken refuge in the clinic of a doctor acquaintance, and has spread the rumor that he is indeed dead. Finally, after a series of unproductive investigations, Wallas decides to inspect Dupont's house, the scene of the crime. At the same time, seven-thirty in the evening 24 hours after the failed attempt on his life, Dupont returns home to pick up some important papers. Seeing Dupont with a gun in his hand, Wallas thinks that the assassin has returned to the crime scene and shoots Dupont dead. Wallas's watch, which had stopped running the day before at seven-thirty, is set in motion again by the recoil of the pistol.

Summarized in this way, *The Erasers* sounds more like a detective story with an ironic twist, along the lines of Agatha Christie's *The Murder of Roger Akroyd*, in which the narrator turns out in the end to be the murderer, than serious fiction of revolutionary import, which is the way the book is made to sound in Barthes's article. Part of the trouble is perhaps that "Objective Literature," which mentions the plot only in order to exclude it from the discussion, is not intended as a totalizing analysis of *The Erasers*. Moreover, although the article is often referred to as being about *The Erasers*, it is based also on some of Robbe-Grillet's early short pieces, *Three Reflected Visions*, which are in fact driven by the purely visual description that Barthes analyzes. If his article had been given a more modest (and uncharacteristic) title such as "Description in Robbe-Grillet's Early Fiction," there would have been less risk that the literary community would get the idea that description is what the novel, and Robbe-Grillet, are about. It should perhaps be said, though, that at the end of the essay Barthes does make some pretty sweeping, even reductive, conclusions:

Robbe-Grillet's purpose . . . is to establish the novel on the surface: once you can set its inner nature, its "interiority," between parentheses, then objects in space, and the circulation of men among them, are promoted to the rank of subjects. The novel becomes man's direct experience of what surrounds him without his being able to shield himself with a psychology, a meta-physic, or a psychoanalytic method in his combat with the objective world he discovers. (p. 27)

At any rate, with this article and the author's own essays that it inspired in part, the *chosiste* Robbe-Grillet was created, to the delight or the consternation of the critical community, depending on one's preferences in literature.

Such was the conventional wisdom about Robbe-Grillet when Bruce Morrissette came on the scene with *Les Romans de Robbe-Grillet* in 1963.[4] Claiming that Barthes's *chosiste* view of *The Erasers* is "a false interpretation," Morrissette chides him for ignoring the novel's plot and, especially, the presence of what Morrissette finds to be the key to the book, allusions to the Oedipus myth.[5]

These allusions, which Barthes in fact does not mention at all, are unmistakable and, especially when one is alerted to them, quite obvious. For example, Wallas punctuates his wanderings through-out the city with unsuccessful attempts to purchase a particular kind of eraser. He once saw the kind he wants at a friend's house; the manufacturer's name was printed on the side but partially worn away, leaving only the middle two letters, "di": Oe*di*pe (p. 126). He sees a set of curtains decorated with the image of shepherds finding an abandoned child (p. 45). A drunk in a bar persists in asking the riddle of the sphinx (p. 13), and a pattern of debris floating in the harbor resembles a "legendary animal: the head, the neck, the breast, the front paws, a lion's body with its long tail, and an eagle's wings" (p. 33). The clinic in which Dupont takes refuge is on Rue de *Corinthe* (p. 70), and in a stationery store Wallas sees a window display representing an artist at work: his painting is of the ruins of Thebes, but the model from which he appears to be working is a photograph of Daniel Dupont's house (pp. 124–25). As for the identity of Oedipus himself, it is Wallas: the agent's peregrinations through the city leave him with swollen feet (p. 251), and he remembers having visited the city as a child, with his mother, on a trip to visit some relative. He at first remembers the relative as being his mother's sister or half-sister (p. 55) but finally remembers that it was a male relative, indeed his father: "How could he have forgotten it?" (p. 231). The police have heard rumors of an estranged son of Daniel Dupont (p. 238), which is enough for the reader to understand the possibilities raised by the "accidental" murder at the end of the book.

The recovery of this evidence is, for Morrissette, refutation of the Barthesian *chosiste* reading, which in Morrissette's view holds Robbe-Grillet to be indifferent to human emotion and the novel to be dominated by minute descriptions of gratuitous objects. Meaning, far from being eliminated or even made problematical in *The Erasers*, as Barthes would have it, is restored: "The story of Wallas in *The Erasers* is a modern version of the tragedy of Oedipus."[6] Critics who suggest that the allusions to the Oedipus story are playful and not to be taken seriously err, according to Morrissette, in reading the novel "superficially"; such an interpretation fails to respect the novel's *unity* and runs the risk of making it *incomprehensible.*[7]

Objects in *The Erasers*, says Morrissette, taking up the challenge posed by Barthes, are not completely devoid of human signification. Taking the eraser as example, Morrissette says that there can be no question of finding in it any mystical link with man; it is not a symbol. It is, however, an objective correlative: objects can become the *supports* for human emotions, as Robbe-Grillet says in *For a New Novel*, and the eraser can be connected with Wallas in several ways. First, in each scene in which Wallas tries to purchase an eraser there is an indication of erotic desire when he finds the saleslady attractive. As it turns out, the saleslady is Daniel Dupont's ex-wife, and while there is no suggestion that she is Wallas's mother, the link is

close enough to suggest Oedipal feelings, and the eraser in consequence becomes "an objective correlative for the important incest
motif."[8] Morrissette also notes that an eraser is in a sense self-
defeating in that it is destroyed in the course of its intended use, an
idea with obvious parallels to the Oedipus story. And finally, the
cube of gum rubber sought by Wallas reminds one of a cube of
stone, a paperweight, on Dupont's desk: "The cube of Dupont (the
father) is large, hard, nonfriable, suitable for protecting papers and
their contents; that of Wallas (the son with the tragic flaw) is soft,
flexible, suitable only for the erasure of writings and drawings, and
achieving its own destruction."[9]

Even the most aggressively resistant of the novel's descriptions,
that of the automat tomato, is made to *signify*, in Morrissette's analysis, however improbably: the slightly torn skin of the tomato that
had been portrayed as "quite faultless" at the beginning of the passage foreshadows Wallas's "tragic flaw."[10]

The last of Barthes's essays on Robbe-Grillet is the preface he
wrote to Morrissette's book.[11] In this preface, he acknowledges, as
he must, that Morrissette identified some legitimate significations
in Robbe-Grillet: the allusions to the Oedipus legend are so obvious
that there is simply no way around them. Barthes makes this
acknowledgment, however, by postulating two Robbe-Grillets: the
first, the *chosiste* "destroyer of meaning" as he appeared in the early
criticism, including Barthes's; the second, the "creator of meaning"
as interpreted by Morrissette.[12] Barthes's assertion is perhaps a tri-
fle slippery, for he in effect attributes to Robbe-Grillet himself the
contradiction between Barthes's and Morrissette's analyses rather
than concludes that one of these analyses, or both, is simply wrong.
Moreover, his assertion is misleading because it is all or nothing: if
one concedes that there is any meaning whatsoever in Robbe-
Grillet's novels, one is obliged according to Barthes to go all the
way to Morrissette's position, which many readers might easily feel
succeeds too well in rendering Robbe-Grillet's universe intelligible.
Barthes calls the second Robbe-Grillet a *humanist*, no less, who is
even "reconciled with the novel's traditional goals," which means
that in Barthes's estimation the author of *For a New Novel* has con-
tradicted himself as few people manage to do.[13]

This is not fair to Robbe-Grillet, and in the last part of his essay
Barthes does (although without postulating a *third* Robbe-Grillet)

say some things that allow for and invite a third point of view. Taken together, the two Robbe-Grillets might be said to "provoke meaning in order to arrest it," to establish a tension in the novels between meaning and nonmeaning.[14] Robbe-Grillet is irretrievably ambiguous, and such ambiguity is perhaps his work's significance and what makes it participate in the underlying function of literature: "What do things signify, what does the world signify? All literature is this question, but we must immediately add, for this is what constitutes its specialty, *literature is this question minus its answer*."[15] Meaning is put in the novels, then, not as a hidden secret for the clever critic to unearth but to raise the problem of meaning itself.

A good many more recent readings of *The Erasers* take this general view of the novel: rather than siding with Barthes or Morrissette in a debate that is in some ways artificial, such critics as Leon Roudiez and Olga Bernal treat the allusions to the Oedipus myth in *The Erasers* not as having a particular meaning but as a reflexive commentary on the *process* of finding meaning. Roudiez, for example, argues that many of the characters in the novel are mythomaniacs. Wallas invents the most complicated justifications to explain his movements in the city: rather than ask a woman in the street for directions to the police station, he asks for instructions to the central post office, thinking it will be near the police station, and invents a telegram he wants to send, so that he ends up arousing the very curiosity he wanted to avoid (pp. 50–52). Robbe-Grillet makes the reader share in this mythomania by dropping clues about Oedipus: Bernal suggests that the clues are just enigmatic enough that the reader can feel proud to have understood them.[16] The reader's interpretive activity parallels Wallas's police work, with equal results in the sense that the Oedipus myth, while certainly present in the story, does not in the end lead anywhere: "the detective is simply no modern Oedipus."[17] The clues leading to the identification of the myth are certain enough, but once one has got them, there is nothing really added to the story except the raw fact that it contains allusions to Oedipus. Even Morrissette, in his recovery of meaning, merely presents his evidence that *The Erasers* is a modern version of the story without specifically relating the myth to the significance of the book any more than that. There is not much to this meaning beyond the deciphering of its signs.

As is so often the case in Robbe-Grillet, the reader will do well to pay attention to certain passages describing the activity of one of the characters in terms that can also mirror the reader's own activity. For example, Wallas's fellow agents have these opinions of their legendary chief, Fabius:

The perspicacity with which he detected the slightest weak point in a suspicious situation, the intensity of impulse that carried him to the very threshold of the enigma, his subsequent indefatigable patience in recomposing the threads that had been revealed, all this seemed to turn at times into the sterile skepticism of a fanatic. Already people were saying that he mistrusted easy solutions, now it is whispered that he has ceased to believe in the existence of any solution whatever. (p. 56)

In this and other ways the novel is reflexive: the reader expects, being conditioned by the realist tradition, to be referred to something outside the text: a reality in which there is a solution to the crime or a message of Oedipal significance, for example, but the text ends up referring to itself and to the very processes by which the reader tries to comprehend it. Wallas's watch, which stops at the start of the story and starts again at the end, represents the delineation of a fictive space, a sequence of events that belongs to the narrative itself more than to the reality the story appears to describe.

This reflexive approach also furnishes a strong reading of the famous descriptions in the novel that is more satisfying than debating whether they conform to existential phenomenology or in what ways an objective correlative is different from a symbol. When one encounters the tomato passage, for example, the intelligibility of the novel, however considerable it may be elsewhere, comes to an abrupt halt. The reader's more or less easy processing of the story is halted peremptorily not so much by a meaningless *tomato* but by a meaningless *description*. The question raised in the reader's mind is not whether tomatoes can have anthropomorphic meaning but what this incongruous description is doing in the middle of a novel that is otherwise not too difficult to follow. Readers conditioned by the traditional novel expect the text to be more or less transparent, leading the reader to the important thing, the story, but Robbe-Grillet's text, through his gratuitous descriptions, asserts its opacity. In this way, as Barthes says, Robbe-Grillet is a *disappointing* writer, one who frustrates the reader's expectations. Or, as Culler puts it, this is

Robbe-Grillet's way of "bringing to our attention the ways we are accustomed to make things intelligible."

Jealousy (1957)

In *Jealousy*, Robbe-Grillet plays on and works against the reader's expectations even more systematically. A small but telling example is the naming of the characters in the novel. The most important character, the jealous husband through whose consciousness the novel is presented, is never named at all. His wife is referred to only by the initial A followed by an ellipsis. Their male neighbor, with whom A . . . may be having an affair, is called Franck, presumably a surname; his wife, who never appears at all, is named Christiane. Now, it is possible to retrieve this unusual system of names, that is, to explain it according to the terms of some reality to which it is thought to conform. Most people probably do not name themselves in their thoughts, at least not very often, and it is perhaps not too shocking that a man should, in his thoughts, designate his wife by something other than her name. "Franck" and "Christiane" are certainly not unusual. But what is more likely going on with the characters' names is not this new kind of realism but a playing on the conventions of the traditional novel. If one accepts that "Franck" is a surname and supposes further that the Francks are a conventional couple, the wife's name is then Christiane Franck, and the continuum is complete: the *less* important the character, the *more* complete a name he or she has. It is exactly the opposite of what is done in most novels and thus exactly the opposite of what the reader expects. When one recalls that Robbe-Grillet protests, in an essay written at the same time as *Jealousy* (*For a New Novel*, 27), against the blind assumption that important characters in novels must have full names, it is very tempting to conclude that in naming his characters he deliberately set out to stand the traditional novel on its head, thereby playing on the reader's expectations.

This matter of what Stephen Heath calls "retrievability" is at the heart of *Jealousy*. Indeed, it is central to all Robbe-Grillet: "The novels of Alain Robbe-Grillet are to be read at the level of their irretrievability, precisely, that is, at the level at which *reading* is posed as a problem and explored as such."[18]

Certainly the question is more acute in *Jealousy* than in, say, *The Erasers*, because the later novel is virtually impossible to read naturally, and this impossibility asserts itself on the very first page. The book opens with a bewildering passage describing a house on a banana plantation in an unspecified French colony:

Now the shadow of the column—the column which supports the southwest corner of the roof—divides the corresponding corner of the veranda into two equal parts. This veranda is a wide, covered gallery surrounding the house on three sides. Since its width is the same for the central portion as for the sides, the line of shadow cast by the column extends precisely to the corner of the house; but it stops there, for only the veranda flagstones are reached by the sun, which is still too high in the sky. (p. 39)

Virtually all the information that the reader has about the house is given in this indirect way, which is quite disconcerting at first. But with some patience the reader can learn to understand this text: he is situated in the consciousness of an observer (identified as the jealous husband, if he is lucky enough to have access to the jacket blurb that Robbe-Grillet eventually suppressed). The "narrative" is in great part the verbal description of the visual images seen or imagined by this central character, whom one would call the narrator if it were clear that the text of the novel is discourse produced by him.

The effect is one of being inside a movie camera, receiving images with as little explanatory information as possible. But once the reader understands the technique, he or she can supply much of the missing information. It is then possible to piece together from the second and third paragraphs that the husband is observing his wife from outside the house, looking at her through an open window. When she turns toward the window, he averts his gaze, turning his head toward the veranda railing so as not to be caught in the act of spying on her:

Now A . . . has come into the bedroom by the inside door opening onto the central hallway. She does not look at the wide open window through which—from the door—she would see this corner of the terrace. Now she has turned back toward the door to close it behind her. . . . The black curls of her hair shift with a supple movement and brush her shoulders as she turns her head.

The heavy hand-rail of the balustrade has almost no paint left on top. The gray of the wood shows through, streaked with tiny longitudinal cracks. (pp. 39–40)

At a certain level, then, the text of *Jealousy* is readable. Once the reader realizes this, he or she may be tempted to apply the process of retrieval on a higher level, and it is in such attempts that (part of) Robbe-Grillet's purpose becomes clear.

As in the case of Robbe-Grillet's explanatory jacket blurb, published and then withdrawn, some of the circumstances of *Jealousy*'s publication reveal useful information about the novel. When the American translation was published in 1959, it appeared with a floor plan of the house, made from the sort of textual clues discussed here. The result is an eminently plausible reconstruction of the house: readers who have experience in tropical colonial settings recognize it at once; Robbe-Grillet, in fact, lived in such a house when he worked in Martinique.[19] Behind the novel's unfamiliar text is a comparatively familiar reality. Indeed, a Balzacian novelist would have said, "It was one of those houses that one sees so often on plantations in ... ," appealing to common knowledge and shared experience, and readers of *Jealousy* might, according to their tastes, feel either irritation or admiration that Robbe-Grillet has accomplished such a familiar descriptive operation in so innovative a way.

But it is exceedingly dangerous to attempt such retrievals of Robbe-Grillet's novel, and on a simple level, the floor plan shows why. The drawing picks up on textual clues very impressively, identifying, among others, the office, the wife's room, the "small bedroom" that the reader can speculate belongs to the husband, with the attendant implications about the state of his relations with his wife. But when all these rooms are added together, one ends up with a blank space on the drawing, an extra room never described in the text, although reference is made to its door. The legend of the floor plan bravely concludes, "Storage room or other (not described)" (p. 37). It is highly ironic—perhaps an irony deliberately invited by Robbe-Grillet—that the reader who wrests from the novel information about the house by means of such close attention to the text must in the end fall back on a purely traditional, Balzacian mode of description that relies on extratextual knowledge and verisimilitude. There *must* be a room there, or the fictional house will not resemble a real one, and it is as likely as anything that it be devoted to storage: the inhabitants must have steamer trunks and the like, since they presumably have traveled to this locale from France and have to put them somewhere. One might as well invent a child or an invalid parent to live in the room; there is equal textual justification—that is, none—for such conclusions.

It would be an ungrateful reader indeed who did not acknowledge how useful the floor plan is and how carefully its maker has read the text. In a sense, however, the plan's greatest utility may be its ultimate failure to reconstruct perfectly a familiar kind of house, for a similar failure awaits efforts to reconstruct more important elements of the novel, such as chronology and action.

And a similar invitation to failure is made by the author, one feels. The unfamiliar description of the house teases the reader into attempting to reconstruct it. The clues that Robbe-Grillet leaves are rather obvious, like the clues to the Oedipus myth in *The Erasers:* the reader who is too inattentive to realize that the angle of the sun's rays on the southwest corner of the house indicates the approximate time of day will surely derive that piece of intelligence from the fact that the sun is *"still too high* in the sky." Robbe-Grillet plays on the reader's expectations and need to retrieve the text of the novel into a familiar, recognizable set of information. These expectations are finally disappointed, and that is Robbe-Grillet's game: there are, in effect, clues to the arrangement of the house's rooms so that one will try, and fail, to draw the floor plan.

So it is, one might feel, with the sequence of events narrated in *Jealousy.* One of the most distinctive features of the novel is the repetition of events, presumably in the husband's memory, coupled with the repetition of *similar* events, until the reader ends up in a chronological jumble. There are several scenes in which Franck, never accompanied by his wife, takes a meal with A . . . and her husband. Again, there are clues that might help the reader separate one meal from another that is very like it: Franck appears sometimes in a white shirt, sometimes in khaki, for example.

But the most noticeable feature of these meal episodes is the most famous scene in the book, the death of a centipede that Franck crushes against the dining room wall. This scene, repeated as many as seven times (although not always in its entirety), acquires a growing significance in the husband's mind, the centipede becoming the objective correlative of his jealousy.

The first iteration is marked by an atmosphere of normality and relative calm (p. 64–65). A . . . and Franck are discussing a shopping trip they plan to make to town; since the town is some distance from the plantation, they will leave early in the morning to be able to return the same evening. A centipede appears on the wall; it is "a common Scutigera of average size."[20] A . . ., who has an aversion to centipedes, cannot look away; her hands are "resting flat on the tablecloth on either side of her plate." When Franck stands up and approaches the wall with his napkin rolled into a ball, "A . . . seems to be breathing faster, but this may be an illusion." As Franck kills the insect, "the hand with the tapering fingers has clenched around the knife handle."

In subsequent repetitions of all or part of this scene, the reader finds increasing agitation and increasingly explicit sexual significance, which peak during a night the husband spends alone in the house; Franck and A . . . do not return from their trip until the following morning. A . . .'s motionless gaze becomes "staring"; in the second scene she is referred to as Franck's "companion." Her hand goes from clenching the knife handle to the tablecloth, then to mosquito netting and finally to a bed sheet: the husband is now imagining, perhaps even hallucinating, the scene as taking place in a hotel room. In the last iteration, the centipede is "enormous: one of the largest to be found in this climate . . . it covers the area of an ordinary dinner plate" (pp. 112–13). Franck kills it with a towel (a pun in French: *serviette* is either "napkin" or "towel"; in this last scene, it is specified that it is a *serviette de toilette*, a towel), and returns to his place, not at table but in bed. The husband's jealousy is at its peak; the centipede has grown along with the husband's emotion. Then, at the end of the novel, he appears to return to a state of relative calm. When A . . . and Franck return the next morning, they explain that Franck's car broke down, that there was no garage open that late, and that they consequently had to stay the night in the hotel. Franck excuses himself for having been a "poor mechanic." In a subsequent conversation, Franck is chattering on about automobile engines, and A . . . interrupts with a remark that seems badly to disconcert him:

"You seem to be up on your mechanics today," A . . . says.
Franck suddenly stops talking, in the middle of his account. He looks at the lips and the eyes on his right, upon which a calm smile, as though with no meaning behind it, seems to be fixed by a photographic exposure. His own mouth has remained half open, perhaps in the middle of a word.
"In theory, I mean," A . . . specifies, without abandoning her most amiable tone of voice. (p. 129)

The reader is free to imagine what all this may imply: perhaps Franck has not been a satisfying lover, but there is no way of know-

ing. What can be known, though, is that the husband's jealousy
seems to have been assuaged: he refers to the car breakdown calmly,
as "an incident of no importance but which postponed their return
to the plantation by a whole night" (p. 128).

So in the confusing jumble of repeated scenes, one thing is quite
easily discernible and very easy to follow: the husband's jealousy
increases steadily to a rage, as shown in the repeated scenes of the
killing of the centipede, and then falls off. The reader will never
know what, if anything, happens between A . . . and Franck but can
follow with some assurance the waxing and waning of the distorting filter of the husband's jealous mind. The title of the novel is significant in this regard: *jalousie* in French means both the emotion
and a kind of slatted window blind, which influences one's perception when one looks through it, just as the emotion of jealousy influences one's perception of events.

Indeed, the rise and fall of jealousy in the book has a completely
classical shape, with tension rising to a climax and falling off in the
denouement. Readers who get this far with *Jealousy* might think that
if so familiar a structure can be extricated from the seeming chaos of
the novel, then further effort, pursuing such things as the different
shirts Franck wears, might eventually succeed in reconstructing the
entire story and, within reason, reveal *what happened*.

Any such attempt is doomed to failure, however. If the rise and
fall of the husband's jealousy can be readily seen, it proves impossible to connect that sequence with a sequence of events lived by the
characters because one comes up against chronological dead ends,
so to speak. For example, it would be quite plausible to suppose that
the husband's jealousy is relatively low before Franck and A . . . plan
their trip, reaches its climax when they fail to return and the husband roams the empty house alone at night, and is calmed when
they do in fact return the next day, with A . . . perhaps teasing
Franck about his inadequacy. But the scene of their return from
town is also among the many repeated scenes, and it first occurs
much *earlier* than the climax of the husband's jealousy, shortly after
the first iteration of the centipede scene. Thus a reconstituted
chronology would associate the husband's growing jealousy with a
scene that occurs after his jealousy has peaked. One could suppose,
of course, that the husband is remembering the entire sequence at
some later time, but that would not fit very well with the powerful
sense of immediacy that each scene gives. Many sections of the

novel begin like the first with the word "Now," and the feeling the reader has is indeed one of being there, in time and space. While a person can *remember* his jealous rages, it seems unlikely that he could *relive* one without some new event setting it off, and in that case it would be reasonable to expect the new fit of jealousy to be connected with the new event. Of course one could imagine that the husband is insane, but to do so would be to buy plausibility at a rather high price.[21]

Rather than attempt to retrieve the plot of *Jealousy*, it makes good sense to treat the rise and fall of jealousy as a written, fictive sequence without trying to reconstruct a story into which it will fit. After all, what would be gained if one were able to sort out the chronology of events, perhaps even decide what happened in the hotel? The novel promises, in its title, to be about jealousy, and so it is, without specifying the exact nature of Franck's relations with A . . . : jealousy is what happens when one *thinks* that one's partner is unfaithful, not necessarily when he or she *is*. Thus the impossibility of reconstructing the plot of *Jealousy* should make the reader realize why he or she wants a reconstructed story so badly: it is largely because readers are accustomed to knowing the story by the long tradition of realist fiction.

The novel concludes with what is perhaps a last reminder of the traditional reader's dependence on plot. Throughout the story, there are a number of spots of one kind or another: the spot on the wall made by the centipede; a spot of oil left by an automobile engine on the stones in the courtyard; the retinal afterimage caused by the bright light of a gasoline lantern. By the end of the novel, the reader is quite used to the relationship between these spots and the subject of the novel: just as jealousy can influence one's perception of events, the retinal afterimage is a defect of vision that alters the images one receives from the real world; the oil spot can be made to disappear by viewing it through a defect in a windowpane. A dramatically new meaning is suggested by the last spot, on the outside wall of the house beneath a window:

The shadow of the column, though it is already very long, would have to be nearly a yard longer to reach the little round spot on the flagstones. From the latter runs a thin vertical thread which increases in size as it rises from the concrete substructure. It then climbs up the wooden surface, from lath to lath, growing gradually larger until it reaches the window sill. . . . On the sill itself, the paint has largely flaked off after the streak occurred, eliminating about three-quarters of the red trace. (pp. 134–35)

The color red is the new element; previously there was mention only of a "dark liquid" (p. 111). Has A . . . been murdered? Perhaps, but the reader should note this possibility only as such, and realize that Robbe-Grillet, for the last time, is playing on the reader's expectations by raising a question that he has no intention of answering.

If one approaches Robbe-Grillet's early novels in this way, as investigations of the problem of intelligibility, there is no contradiction between a *chosiste* and a humanist Robbe-Grillet. Rather than eliminating meaning in *The Erasers* only suddenly to discover it in *Jealousy*, Robbe-Grillet in both novels holds meaning and nonmeaning in dynamic tension. Certainly there is evolution from one novel to the next, and no one would say that Robbe-Grillet merely repeats himself; but when one considers what the two novels have in common, a fundamental coherence emerges. In both, a character pursues an enigma without ever finding a solution, and the reader is invited to pursue a certain kind of understanding without being allowed to succeed. From both failures, the characters' and the reader's, one learns certain things about the process of understanding.

Djinn/Le Rendez-vous (1981)

A good many of Robbe-Grillet's later works are not novels, strictly speaking. He has been heavily involved in the cinema, and many of his print works of the 1970s are what Bruce Morrissette calls "intertextual assemblages."[22] Some of these, such as *Topologie d'une cité fantôme* (1975) and *Souvenirs du triangle d'or* (1978), are composed of passages of text published in other works, many of which are books containing text by Robbe-Grillet accompanied by the work of such artists as Jasper Johns, René Magritte, and Robert Rauschenberg, and the photographers David Hamilton and Irina Ionesco.

Falling into this category of mixed genres, perhaps, is *Le Rendez-vous*, published in French in the United States as a language textbook, with text by Robbe-Grillet and grammatical exercises by Yvone Lenard, the author of several successful American textbooks for teaching French. The same work was published the same year in France as *Djinn* (the English translation is also *Djinn*), a novel, more or less, without the pedagogical apparatus. The work thus is informed by (at least) two genres, the creative novel and the foreign-language reader. Moreover, *Djinn* adds to the text of *Le Rendez-vous* a prologue and an epilogue that purport to present the text of *Le Rendez-vous* as a found manuscript, and in the prologue Robbe-Grillet states that the manuscript is difficult to classify: it resembles "pure fiction" but also a textbook, but the apparent pedagogical nature of the text may also be a "mere guise" for something else.[23]

The intersection of the novel and other genres in *Djinn* allows Robbe-Grillet to expand the range of his explorations of intelligibility and readerly expectation. Although his earlier novels certainly touch on language as an organizing principle of human understanding, the relationship of French and English in a text aimed at American students invites specific, bilingual play. Indeed, the title *Djinn* is based on such a play: in chapter one, the protagonist and (sometime) narrator, Simon Lecoeur, goes to meet a person known to him only as Jean. Assuming the name is French, he expects a man: "Monsieur Jean, I presume?" but he is answered by a woman, who corrects his pronunciation (this is, after all, a foreign-language textbook): "Do not pronounce it *Jean*, but Djinn. I am an American" (p. 12). In this respect as in others, the character Simon exemplifies the problem of expectation and intelligibility: being French, he expects Jean from its spelling to be a man's name and so is prepared to meet a man; when he arrives at the meeting place he sees a figure dressed in a trench coat, which he immediately interprets against another cultural background, the 1930s crime film, which further reinforces his expectation that the person is a man. When his interlocutor turns out to be the American woman Jean, it is only the first of many frustrated expectations.

Moreover, the text of *Djinn* was written specifically to be a foreign-language reader, so grammatical structure is one of the organizing principles of the text. The book begins with relatively simple French and proceeds to more and more complex structures, which tend to come in concentrated lessons: for example, when one comes to what is obviously the lesson on the subjunctive, there are sentences with three or four subjunctives, illustrating different uses of the structure. The concentration of structures is such that even the reader of the nontextbook version of the novel will notice it and realize that the story is not the only driving force behind the text. There results an effect that is perhaps comparable to the textual opacity asserted by the objective descriptions in *The Erasers:* the reader's attention is drawn to the very texture of the book rather than passing with relative ease through the language of the text to the story, as conventional expectations would have it.

The multiple genres suggested by *Djinn* also let Robbe-Grillet build on an effect he produced previously in *The Erasers* and *Jealousy.* To the extent that the reader is conscious of genre in reading the work, the realist goal of delivering story through a relatively transparent vehicle is lost. The reader's awareness of genre accentuates the formal underpinnings of the work, the conventions by which it is constructed. *The Erasers* and *Jealousy* produce this effect by appearing to belong to a well-known genre (the murder mystery, the love-triangle story) yet failing to deliver everything the reader is entitled to (the identity of the murderer, the truth behind the jealous passion). That is, these two novels encourage a certain set of expectations only in order to frustrate them, thus calling to the reader's attention the conventional nature of those expectations. *Djinn* accomplishes a similar aim by refusing to engage clearly with any genre, or, rather, by self-consciously engaging with several different genres without following through on any of them. The characters themselves refer to various genres as they try to understand what is happening to them. As mentioned above, Simon recognizes the figure in the trench coat as belonging to a certain kind of film; later, he compares himself to an actor in a play (pp. 37–38), almost falls down in a heap with the boy Jean "like characters out of Samuel Beckett" (p. 90), and talks with a girl named Marie, who discloses her ambition to study to be the heroine of a novel: "It is a good job, and it allows one to live in the literary style" (p. 48). At one point he has the feeling that another character is reciting a lesson, which of course she is, since the book in which Simon is a character is a foreign-language textbook (p. 35). To decide to what genre the story belongs would be to make much progress in understanding it, but that understanding is denied both the characters and the reader.

Similarly, in *Djinn* Robbe-Grillet explores some of the same techniques of the novel that he did in his earlier works, to much the same effect but in perhaps a more radical way. *Jealousy,* for example, raises the issue of narrative technique by limiting the point of view to the jealous husband so systematically that the reader may at first be unable to comprehend what Robbe-Grillet is doing. Although the novel's narrative stance can finally be understood and even justified as being faithful to a certain reality, *Jealousy* may be said to question traditional narrative practices by making its use of focalized narration such a tour de force as to test the limits of the technique. *Djinn* draws attention to the subject of narration by starting in a fairly conventional way, with Simon as first-person narrator, then switching abruptly and without explanation to a conventional third-person narrative at the start of chapter 6, only to switch back to Simon, again without explanation, 12 pages later (p. 84). And in the final chapter, which resembles the first in many ways, the narrator suddenly becomes a woman. In this respect as in nearly all others, the novel asserts itself as a fiction, using novelistic devices not in order to better portray some "reality" but for their own sake.

From one perspective, then, *Djinn* may be said to contest the idea of realist, or even merely referential, fiction. The reader can have no hope of discovering a reality behind the novel; rather, the novel utterly frustrates conventional readerly expectations by radically and aggressively pointing to itself and its own construction. But such is approximately the significance of *Jealousy*, not to mention *The Erasers* and several of Robbe-Grillet's other early novels, and the fact that the author delivers the same message in 1981 as in 1957, albeit with expanded techniques for delivering that message, invites the charge that Robbe-Grillet is content simply to repeat a set of tricks.[24] Moreover, directing one's energies against the Balzacian novel in 1981 is like swinging after the bell: that particular model of novelistic practice has been thoroughly undermined since the 1950s, not the least by Robbe-Grillet himself. Indeed, one is sometimes tempted to conclude that the New Novelists in general are reactive rather than proactive, more obsessed with overturning the traditional novel more than interested in creating truly new possibilities for fiction.

But by the late 1970s and 1980s, Robbe-Grillet's fiction has other avowed goals in addition to his opposition to the traditional novel and the ideology it implies, and it may be the critic, not the author, who is guilty of repeating a set of tricks by reading *Djinn* as another deconstruction of nineteenth-century fiction and nothing more. The ideas about man, the world, and the novel that he expresses so forcefully in *For a New Novel* and that inform many of his early creative works are not what interests him most in his writing; Robbe-Grillet has "nothing to say":

Thus the novel's content . . . can actually only consist in the banality of the always-already-said: a string of stereotypes lacking originality by definition. The only meanings are those established in advance by society. But these "received ideas" (which we now call ideology) will nevertheless be the only possible material for the construction of a work of art—novel, poem, essay—empty architecture entirely held up by its form. The substance and originality of the text will come solely from the organization of its elements, which are of no interest in themselves.[25]

The idea of a novel held up by form alone is not new, nor is this the first time that this Flaubertian idea appears in Robbe-Grillet's work. But of the three novels discussed here, *Djinn* is the one that gives the best idea of what a novel made of form would look like: *The Erasers* and *Jealousy* are certainly formal innovations, but they are very much *arguments* as well.

Much of the text of *Djinn* seems to be generated by variations in the organization of textual elements, which Robbe-Grillet calls *glissements* ("slippages"): "The movement of literature is this slippage of a scene to the same scene repeated in a form that is barely diverted, barely skirted, barely turned around."[26] This description sounds a great deal like some of the repeated scenes in *Jealousy*, the most dramatic example being the evolution of the centipede scene. But the modification of repeated scenes in the earlier novel is *motivated:* the reader understands that the modifications are charged with meaning and that the whole process is explainable by the associations of an obsessional mind.

In *Djinn*, the only motivation appears to be compositional, and the process resembles a kind of internal intertextuality whereby the text in effect echoes itself. David Walker cites as examples two scenes, the first being the one in which Simon goes to meet Djinn at the warehouse, the second the one in which he takes the unconscious boy to a house. The italicized portions of each text show the slippage process:

Under the *dim light* that filters through the large windows with dirt-encrusted, partly broken panes, *I can barely make out* the objects that surround me, piled on all sides in great disarray, no doubt cast off: ancient discarded machinery, metallic carcasses, and *assorted old hardware*, which dust and rust darken to a blackish and uniformly dull tint . . . *a pile of oddly shaped crates*. (pp. 11–12)

This is where the *faint light* comes from. . . . *It allows me to make out* the shapes of the furniture . . . three or four *unmatched chairs*, their seats more or less caved in, an *iron* bedstead and *a large number of trunks of various shapes and sizes.* (pp. 26–27)

The echoing here is based not on meaning but on repeated words, repeated sounds, and associations of words (crates and trunks, for example). The process indeed owes more to poetry than to representational fiction, and the result has in common with poetry the primacy accorded to form rather than to content.

The intertextuality extends to other texts by Robbe-Grillet. There are, for example, a number of echoes of *Jealousy* in *Djinn*: Djinn reminds Simon of an actress named Jane *Frank,* which might suggest the Franck of the earlier novel, and certain sentences could be almost lifted from *Jealousy:* "The whole house is plunged into total silence, as though abandoned" (p. 27). There are even references to Oedipus, which recalls *The Erasers,* although the following passage seems to be more a deliberate reminiscence than a *glissement:* Simon, disguised as a blind man and being led by two children, thinks to himself, "I must have one hell of an Oedipus complex" (p. 84). But Oedipal complexes are even less applicable to *Djinn* than to *The Eraser,* as is perhaps suggested by Simon's rather inappropriate association of the Oedipal complex with the end of the Oedipus story rather than with his killing his father. In any case, the message of all these intertextual echoes seems clear: what generates them is formal or even poetic association rather than some hidden meaning to be ferreted out by the reader.

Djinn shows Robbe-Grillet's interests evolving. He has not abandoned his early convictions about the traditional novel; like *The Erasers, Jealousy,* and other of his novels, *Djinn* attacks the underlying assumptions of traditional fiction. But Robbe-Grillet also goes beyond his earliest preoccupations to a new phase in his exploration of writing. It is on this ground—the exploration of writing—that Robbe-Grillet is best defended against his detractors. His theoretical statements about the novel are certainly provocative and in many cases highly insightful, but one is struck in his theoretical writings—both in *For a New Novel* and in later texts, mostly published interviews—by an inability to follow certain of his contemporaries into the complexities of advanced theoretical thought.

Fortunately, Robbe-Grillet's imaginative work is both richer and more coherent than some of his theory. It is not that the theory has little to do with the novels and should be avoided: the interplay between essay and novel is one of the real pleasures of reading him.

Though the relationship between theory and fiction is often a very close one, it is only seldom if at all that the reader has the impression either that the theory is only an explanation of the novels, or that the novels are written merely to illustrate the theory. Rather, the two sides of Robbe-Grillet's enterprise illuminate each other, the creative work explaining the theory as often as not in the sense that it is in the novels that Robbe-Grillet's project is most coherent.

4

Nathalie Sarraute

Unlike Robbe-Grillet's, Nathalie Sarraute's career was rather slow in gathering momentum. She began writing before the other New Novelists: *Tropisms*, written between 1932 and 1937, was finally published in 1939.[1] The book attracted relatively little notice. During the early 1940s, she wrote more "tropisms," but they were not published until 1957, when Editions de Minuit reissued *Tropisms* with the later texts added to the original. Her next book, *Portrait d'un inconnu* (*Portrait of a Man Unknown*), after being rejected once or twice, was finally published in 1948 by the new firm of Robert Marin. After only 400 copies had been sold, the publisher disposed of the rest. Her next novel, *Martereau* (1953), attracted rather more attention, but her career had still not progressed to the level that it would ultimately attain. In 1947, Sarraute began writing critical articles, the first few appearing in Sartre's *Les Temps modernes*, again without causing much comment. When these articles were collected as *The Age of Suspicion* in 1956, however, Sarraute was surprised that they attracted much more attention; by then, of course, the controversy over the New Novel was beginning to boil. Robbe-Grillet reviewed the book in *Critique*, and the two writers met.[2] Sarraute has always freely acknowledged the boost given to her career by her association with the New Novel and Robbe-Grillet. *Le Planétarium* (*The Planetarium*), published in 1959, was praised as an example of the New Novel, and *Les Fruits d'or* (*The Golden Fruits*) won the International Prize for Literature in 1963. After *Entre la vie et la mort* (*Between Life and Death*) in 1968, she turned her attention to drama, writing a number of radio plays. Her later novels include *Vous les entendez?* (*Do You Hear Them?*; 1972), *Disent les imbéciles* (*Fools Say*; 1976), *L'Usage de la parole* (1980), and *Tu ne t'aimes pas* (*You Don't Love Yourself*; 1989).

There is considerable continuity to Sarraute's work. She herself stated that the concept of tropism was at the heart of all her books. Her first postwar book is a most interesting elaboration of the themes announced in *Tropisms*.

Portrait of a Man Unknown (1948)

If in *Tropisms* Nathalie Sarraute's purpose was to illustrate her notion of the undercurrents of emotional life, in *Portrait of a Man Unknown* she *dramatized* her ideas by creating a character (also the narrator) who seeks out evidence of tropistic activity in other people, who encounters other characters who dispute his psychological notions, and who at times is unsure whether he is right. The result is much more like a novel than the earlier work, with a sustained plot of sorts and characters who appear in the book from beginning to end, although most of them are still without names. *Portrait of a Man Unknown* is a more dynamic work as well, since the tropistic view of human relationships is opposed by characters who have more traditional opinions, and from this opposition one gains a clearer view of Sarraute's convictions and their relation to other modes of thought.

Portrait of a Man Unknown* may be more of a novel than *Tropisms*, but that does not mean that it is traditional in form or that it is especially transparent. The reader is likely to be quite perplexed at the beginning: the following passage begins on the novel's first page, and although many of the central themes are present in it, one does not know this until much later:

I began by being matter of fact and natural, in order not to frighten them. I asked them if they didn't sense, as I did, if occasionally they hadn't sensed something queer, a vague something that emanated from her and clung to them . . . but they snubbed me immediately, cutting me short, as usual, pretending not to understand: "She's a bit tiresome," they answered, "a bit of a bore . . ." I hung on: "Don't you think . . ." already my voice was giving out, it didn't sound true—in such moments one's voice never sounds true, it hesitates as it hunts around for a tone; having, in its confusion, mislaid its own, it tries to assume one that is plausible, well assured, respectable—in a voice that was too flat, too colorless, and which must have betrayed me, I tried to insist: "didn't they think, hadn't they occasionally sensed something that she exuded, something soft and gluey that stuck to them and inhaled them, without their knowing quite how, something they had to take hold of and tear off their skins, like a damp compress with a stale, sweetish odor. . . ." This was dangerous, going too far, which they detested.[3]

As one continues to read, the characters alluded to here become clear. There are two groups referred to as "they" or "them" in this passage: first, unnamed persons with whom the narrator attempts to discuss the second group referred to as "them," an old man and his daughter, in whom the narrator senses the hidden emotional stirrings that Sarraute calls tropisms.

What is immediately evident is that two fundamentally different views of human life are opposed here: whereas the narrator's interlocutors are inclined to label the father and daughter as "miser" and "spinster," the narrator has a vague but persistent feeling that they have indefinable qualities. The most he can get from his acquaintances, however, is a dismissive judgment: the daughter is "a bit of a bore." It is important that these different views are manifested by different uses of language: the narrator cannot easily put his feeling into words, whereas the others are able to put an end to all ambiguity with an aptly chosen word: "Yet one word from them, just one of those quick words that shoot forth from them and land in exactly the right place, like a boxer's blow, one word such as they occasionally know how to utter, would have kept me quiet for a while" (p. 18). This passage illustrates Sarraute's conviction that the naming of psychological qualities and relationships is a falsification, a handy convention that we use instead of looking for the real truth. Declarative language seems to deal in essences, and thus has enormous power: "Then I realize that's it. I acknowledge their blinding perspicacity. It bowls me over; shining, convincing, absolutely irrefutable and terrible, it falls on me with a thud and lays me out flat as I listen, motionless, on the landing below, to their infallible judgment, their verdict" (p. 19). The violent vocabulary of these two passages ("shoot forth," "boxer's blow," "lays me out flat") shows the power of language—the power to do violence to reality. The father has the habit (as does one of the characters in *Tropisms*) of asking rapid-fire questions that reduce his interlocutor to embarrassed silence, as when he inquires about the narrator's plans: "Greece? The Parthenon? Eh? Museums? The Eleusinian Mysteries? Have you been to Eleusis? Art? Florence? Pictures? The Uffizi? You've seen all that? Eh?" (p. 38).

This world of certainty registered in words and names is for most people the real world; the narrator's view is peculiar to him. That is no doubt why he shows such lack of confidence in his own intuitions, but his is a diffidence that Sarraute does not share: here and in other novels the narrator and the author may have certain qualities in common, but one should not conclude that these novels are autobiographical. In *Portrait of a Man Unknown* the narrator gropes for a vision of human relationships that Sarraute, for her part, has already attained. The tension created by the narrator's lack of conviction, however, serves to clarify the issues involved.

In the fourth section of the novel, the narrator, who has had very mixed feelings about his preoccupations, decides that his obsessive interest in the emotional secrets of the father and daughter is threatening to get the better of him, and "gives up," as he puts it, deciding to see a "specialist." This figure is at least partly a psychiatrist: the emotional stirrings that so fascinate the narrator are "in his department" (p. 73). The cure the narrator seeks is to gain the sense of certainty that his interlocutors of the opening section have. That is the function of specialists: "They straighten all that out in no time and pigeonhole it in their own way. That private little idea, or that private little vision of yours that you had been brooding over with mingled pride and shyness, is labeled and tossed in among others in the same category" (p. 72). As a result of the specialist's advice, the narrator feels that he is beginning to be cured of his obsession with the father and daughter and to get a grip on reality. The father and daughter are losing their vagueness for him: "They have come nearer and are growing hard and finished, with clear colors and distinct outlines, only rather like the painted cardboard dolls that serve as targets in street fairs. One more click of the trigger and down they'll fall" (p. 74).

The first edition of *Portrait of a Man Unknown* was published with a preface by Sartre, who had been one of the few to respond favorably to *Tropisms*. This essay is interesting in its own right—it was here that Sartre formulated his notion of "antinovel"—and also helps illuminate Sarraute's novel. Indeed, it is very tempting to talk about the two visions that are opposed in the novel in terms of existential ontology. The characters who are given to attaching labels to people, whether they are gossips or "specialists," do so because they believe, if only implicitly, in essences. They talk as if reality itself were divided into the categories provided by language, as if a hard core of immutable Being were at the heart of every existing thing.

There are numerous similarities between *Portrait of a Man Unknown* and Sartre's *Nausea*. In a minor passage in the latter, the narrator Roquentin witnesses a scene of judgment through language that is quite reminiscent of some of the dismissive judgments in *Portrait of a Man Unknown*. In the following passage, the self-assured, domineering Dr. Rogé enters a restaurant and sees a timid little man whom he knows:

> "So it's you, you old swine," he shouts, "aren't you dead yet?"
> He addresses the waitress:
> "You let people like that in here?"
> He stares at the little man ferociously. A direct look which puts everything in place. He explains:
> "He's a crazy old loon, that's that."
> He doesn't even take the trouble to let on that he's joking. He knows the loony won't be angry, that he's going to smile. And there it is: the man smiles with humility. A crazy loon: he relaxes, he feels protected against himself: nothing will happen to him today. I am reassured too. A crazy old loon: so that was it, so that was all.[4]

The world of Being is so comfortable and reassuring that it does not matter to the little man *what* he is, so long as he *is something*, with finality and certitude.

The two novels do not deal with precisely the same subject matter: Sartre is interested in ontology, as illustrated by Roquentin's discovery of formless Existence as opposed to Being, whereas Sarraute is talking about human psychology. But the topics are related, and the imagery the two authors use to discuss the opposing concepts is quite similar. In *Nausea* the world of Being is hard, solid, and massive. Its opposite, the world of Existence, is soft, sticky, viscous, and half liquid (the name of the city in which the book is set, Bouville, suggests "Mud City"). Sarraute exploits the same imagery in *Portrait of a Man Unknown*. In the essays contained in *The Age of Suspicion* she systematically favors images of interiority at the expense of the exterior. What relates her imagery and Sartre's is that in Sarraute's novels, the interior, like Roquentin's visions of Existence, is soft and sticky: "And then I feel a strange substance trickling from them in an endless stream, a substance as anonymous as lymph, or blood, an insipid liquid that flows through my hands and spills" (p. 69). The exterior of human beings, psychologically speaking, is for Sarraute a "mask," "shell," or "carapace" designed to shield them from the emotional demands of others, which are often represented by "tentacles" or "suckers." These images occur throughout the novel, most significantly to describe the relationship of father and daughter: "A mask—that is the word I always use, although it is not exactly suitable, to describe the expression he assumes as soon as she comes in. . . . Immediately, as though actuated by some sort of automatic trigger, his face changes: it grows heavy and taut, taking on the very special, artificial, stiff expression that people often have when they look at themselves in the mirror" (p. 61). The narrator imagines that the father must have been like that when he first saw his newborn daughter. Tiny infants may seem innocent, but beneath external appearances they have "delicate little suckers like those that stretch, trembling, on the end of the hairs that line carnivorous plants" (p. 62). This is the "terrible need to establish contact" that Katherine Mansfield found in Dostoevsky's characters and that Sarraute comments on in *The Age of Suspicion,* and the armor that people use to shield themselves from this demand.

Sartre concludes his preface by suggesting that *Portrait of a Man Unknown* "makes it possible to attain, over and beyond the psychological, human reality in its very *existence*" (p. xiv). While Sarraute's affinity with Sartre may not be quite as complete as that, it is true that both *Nausea* and *Portrait of a Man Unknown* portray a narrator caught between two worlds, one reassuring but inauthentic, the other authentic but frightening.

One of the most important aspects of *Portrait of a Man Unknown* is the relationship between the narrator and models of literary creation. The theme is explicitly stated when the narrator observes that his notion of the mask reminds him of Prince Bolkonski, the "well-drawn," "vivid" character in *War and Peace* (p. 64). As the narrator knows, the great characters of Realist fiction are commonly held to be "real," to seem "alive"—so real, he says ironically, as to seem more alive than actual living people (p. 67). Thus Sarraute's interest in the theory of the novel joins with the theme of authentic and inauthentic views of human existence: the conventional standard for realistic fictional characters—that they be consistent, perfectly formed and knowable—is such that real human beings would not qualify. Worse, under the influence of fiction, we begin to perceive people in our own lives as we do fictional characters: "each one of them appears to us as a finished, perfect whole, entirely enclosed on every side, a solid, hard block, without a single fissure, a smooth sphere that offers nothing the hand can grasp" (pp. 67–68). The narrator's problem is that when presented with such smooth surfaces, his obsession is such that he must "try with fanatical eagerness to find the crack" (p. 69).

It is at this point that the narrator consults the specialist, and brings up the matter of Prince Bolkonski. The specialist has conventional ideas about literary representation, believing that the role of art is to "clothe abstraction" (p. 75). As part of the "cure," he gives the narrator advice for his relationships with people that is precisely the advice that used to be given to aspiring novelists for the treatment of character: "But make him live first, make him concrete, tangible" (p. 75). Sarraute's point is clear, as she wrote in 1960: "I chose [characters from *War and Peace*] in order to oppose them, in their perfection, to what fictional characters had become, after all the dislocations and disintegrations they had undergone in the contemporary novel. I wanted to show that trying to imitate these models would be to disregard the evolution of literature in our time."[5]

Sarraute made the same point on a more implicit level by choosing a father-daughter pair that every student of French literature recognizes as resembling the main characters of Balzac's *Eugénie Grandet*. Thus the central tension in *Portrait of a Man Unknown* takes on a theoretical meaning: if the old man and his daughter turn out really to be no more than the well-drawn figures that the others see in them, the Balzacian novel will be vindicated. If, on the other hand, the narrator is right, then modern writers should take a different approach to fiction.

The "cure" works for a while, and the narrator manages to go about his business in the "serene world of distinctly drawn outlines" that everyone else seems to live in (p. 80). Travel is the usual prescription for a person undergoing such a recovery, and he makes a trip to a Dutch city.

There he visits a museum, where his attitude changes again. Most of the paintings have a "salutary" effect on him, advancing his "cure" since they are finished works of graceful line. But one painting in particular, entitled *Portrait of a Man Unknown*, by an anonymous painter, takes hold of him and reawakens his old preoccupations. The painting seems unfinished, with "fragmentary, uncertain outlines," and reminds the narrator of a corpse caught by death in the midst of some activity, that is, of something profoundly alive until transfixed by the painting (p. 84). Only the eyes seem finished, yet they appear not quite to belong to the face. Clearly the authentic world, ill defined but vitally real, is reasserting itself.

It is also art that asserts itself. The painting is directly opposed to the other, finished paintings, but also to the Prince Bolkonskis of realist fiction. The entire episode takes place intertextually, under the sign of literary art. The narrator refers to this city only as the city of Baudelaire's "Invitation au voyage" (in which case it is in Holland); the sudden feeling of liberation he has reminds one of any number of Proustian epiphanies, and the image with which he concludes the section, of a ship suddenly cut free from the land, sailing toward the open sea, is perhaps an allusion to Rimbaud's famous poem "Le Bateau ivre." His language in the pages that follow the description of the painting is more imagistic, more "literary."

Henceforth, the narrator will pursue his visions more as a creative writer than as a frustrated observer.[6] It is not that he has literally become a writer, but the avenue of approach to his subjects has become scenes that are effectively imaginary, or at least scenes that he does not witness directly. The old man becomes more and more the chief representative of the ordinary world of certainty, and thus the narrator's chief antagonist. The narrator has some early successes: in one passage, he reconstructs a scene that must have transpired during an outing of the old man and some of his friends, when the old man blurts out a hysterical condemnation of his daughter and all ungrateful children, but he still has the feeling that something is eluding him.

What has been eluding him is revealed in a long climactic scene, presumably imagined since the narrator cannot have witnessed it, between the father and daughter. It is a scene of confrontation, in which the different sets of opposing forces in the novel all clash in battle: father against daughter, the narrator against the father-daughter couple, the tropistic world against the world of stable meanings, the new novel against the old.

The confrontation begins when the daughter asks her father for money she needs for medical treatments. At first, the two argue in their fixed, normal-world identities of miser and demanding daughter: "awkward, in their rigid carapaces, their heavy armor—two giant insects, two enormous dung beetles" (p. 174). In support of these established identities, the narrator cites the two characters' "support groups." The daughter has a circle of friends who give her moral support with their pronouncements regarding her father: "and when you think that she's all he has in the world . . . one thing is certain, he can't take it with him" (p. 169). The father, for his part, has a circle of friends whom he meets for dinner; they, of course, furnish him with clichés about ungrateful children and the softness of the modern generation. Making it clear that what is at stake is more than simple clichés, however, Sarraute writes that in the company of his cronies, the old man acquires an entirely different mode of being: "Under their placid gaze, a manner they have that is so self-assured and always slightly indifferent, he felt that he filled up with a consistent substance that gave him density and weight, steadiness, he too became 'somebody,' protected and respectable, deeply rooted, stuck like a wedge in the well-constructed universe they lived in" (p. 170).

The quarrel escalates to a truly remarkable intensity when the father switches from the theme of the ungrateful child to berate his daughter for her ugliness and unmarriageability. As this happens, however, the relationship between the two antagonists begins to change. Their masklike roles break up and they are drawn into a tropistic world, leaving the familiar one far behind: "they were naked, without protection, they were slipping, clasped to each other, they were going down as into the bottom of a well . . . the fairies, the old cronies, already far behind, had remained up there, on the surface, in the daylight . . . down where they were going now, things seemed to wobble and sway as in an undersea landscape, at once distinct and unreal, like objects in a nightmare" (p. 176). The two antagonists are now functioning as tropistic entities, so to speak, sharing a relationship different from the one seen in the surface world. The narrator finally has confirmation of his intuitions about the couple, even if the confirmation is imaginary, his own creation.

Confirmation of what, exactly? What *is* this tropistic relationship underlying the father's and daughter's surface identities? It is difficult to say, and rightly so, because Sarraute's theory holds that the *naming* of emotional states in conventional terms is a falsification. Often, in the pages devoted to this scene in the novel, she asserts that something is happening without saying exactly what. When she does try to make the reader see, her method is evocative rather than descriptive:

the abscess had burst, the scab was entirely off, the wound was bleeding, suffering and voluptuousness had attained their peak, he was at the end of his tether, at the very end, they had reached bottom, alone together, they were by themselves, now they were quite by themselves, naked, stripped, far from outside eyes . . . he felt steeped in the atmosphere of mellowness, the relaxed tepidity produced by intimacy—alone in their nice, big hideout, where you can do anything you want . . . (p. 188)

Those who are not bound by the strictures of Sarraute's theory might say that what is revealed in this long scene is the bond between father and daughter that underlies their surface hatred; this hypothesis is perhaps strengthened when at the end of the scene the father gives his daughter 4,000 francs, this after reaching levels of venom that make the reader wonder that he didn't kill her. She had requested 6,000, but her relief and satisfaction are such that the reader may very well understand that her request was inflated so as to allow for a reduction, and that this scene has repeated itself many times between the two. But Sarraute has won her point: an easy label does not do justice to the power of the scene.

After this paroxysm of tropistic activity, one might expect the narrator to rejoice in his discovery, but that is not what happens. Rather, the last pages of the novel undo what one feels was nevertheless the author's main point, as the "common sense" world of fixed Being reasserts itself.

At the end of their quarrel, the daughter triumphantly (and spitefully) announces to her enraged father that in spite of everything she is engaged to be married. The novel concludes with a conversation among the old man, his daughter, the narrator, and the fiancé. The latter is alone among all the important characters in having a name: Louis Dumontet. Names, of course, belong to Sarraute's "normal" world, and Dumontet is an emissary from that world; he is not physically impressive, but is so at home in the real world that the narrator describes him in these terms: "Extremely sure of himself. Unperturbed. Imposing. A rock. A cliff that has resisted all the onslaughts of the ocean. Unassailable. A compact block. All smooth and hard" (p. 209). Faced with such solidity, it is the authentic world of tropisms that gives way: the narrator barely recognizes the daughter, who has shed the black stockings of her spinsterhood and acquired a "smooth, flawless look, that sort of set glamor" (p. 208).

As the conversation progresses, Dumontet presents his plans for refurbishing a country home, doing some fishing, and growing apples. The narrator, that erstwhile hypersensitive interested only in pursuing tropisms, finds himself making such mundane observations as "Apple trees are the principal trees of that region. My uncle used to make cider that was as good as the best Normandy cider" (p. 217), and ends up debating with Dumontet whether trolling or live bait is the best method of catching pike.

How is one to understand this reversal? Some readers have concluded that the narrator's vision is inauthentic, even when he thinks he is succeeding, and that his final capitulation is meant to show his failure. But this view does not explain the triumphant success of the quarrel scene, the most compelling in the book, nor is it a necessary conclusion. The victory at the end of the novel of the normal, real world over the tropistic vision has more to do with the nature of tropisms than with the qualifications of their champion, the narrator. Sarraute's tropisms are by nature elusive, fragmentary, and impressionistic; the "real" world of certainty always imposes itself over this fleeting vision. It makes no difference that the "real" world is actually false.

For if the narrator in fact yields to Dumontet at the end of the novel, he has not lost his convictions. He will capitulate, he will call the old man "egoist" and "miser," but he is under no delusion that this is the way life really is:

Little by little everything will grow calm. The world will take on a smooth, clean, purified aspect. Somewhat akin to the air of serene purity that the faces of people are always said to assume after death.
   After death . . .? But that, too, is nothing, either. Even that rather strange look, as though things were petrified, that slightly lifeless look, will disappear in time. Everything will be all right. . . . It will be nothing. . . . Just one more step to be taken. (p. 223)

Between Life and Death (1968)

The Planetarium and *The Golden Fruits* won a wider audience for Sarraute but also led to serious questions about her goals in writing fiction. *The Planetarium* deals with a young couple in search of an apartment in fashionable Paris; *The Golden Fruits* is about a novel, "Les Fruits d'or," and its reception by Parisian literary society. A number of influential readers have concluded that, far from pursuing the elementary structures of human relationships, Sarraute in these two novels has produced comedies of manners. Sartre, who supported Sarraute at the start of her career, revised his early opinion somewhat: "she thinks that through the protoplasmic exchanges that she describes she attains fundamental individual relationships, whereas all she does is show the abstract, infinitesimal effects of a sharply defined social milieu."[7] Other critics have likened her work to that of George Eliot or Jane Austen, and have concluded that the greatest gift displayed in these two novels is a keen ear for the intonations of fashionable Paris.[8]

Between Life and Death answers many of these criticisms. The novel drew high praise and constitutes an important juncture in Sarraute's career. The subject of the book is once again a novel, but rather than focus on the novel as a social artifact, this time she is at pains to get at the creative act itself. The tropistic stirrings that *Between Life and Death* attempts to convey to the reader are those of literary composition.

There is a narrative structure to the book: the different sections, unnumbered as they always are in Sarraute's work, trace the creation of a nameless writer's first novel from his childhood to the point at which he begins work on his second. The narrative is less traditional than that of *Portrait of a Man Unknown*, however, in that the reader cannot be at all certain that all the stages deal with the same writer. Is the mature writer of the first section who somewhat fatuously declares, "I tear out the page . . . I throw it away. I take another sheet. I write" (p. 1) the same as the one Sarraute shows in the other sections? As in *Portrait of a Man Unknown*, there are no proper names to guide the reader, but here Sarraute goes even further by introducing in the same paragraph a slippage in the use of personal pronouns: "I" and "you" in the same paragraph can be the same person.

Sarraute's ear is as keen as ever; there are elements of social satire that echo *The Golden Fruits*. Midway through the book, the writer suffers through an exposition by a university professor of literature, who has discovered in his novel things that utterly elude the author:

[The writer] is leaning forward, he is straining, he is opening up to take in the words that will follow. . . . There's a minute of silence . . . he would like to break it off, he would like to prolong it just a little . . . just one more moment of suspense . . . but there they are . . . they are coming out in brief jerks . . . words with no visible connection between them . . . they are falling thick and fast, they drum against him without penetrating. From time to time he succeeds in catching some in passing: Symbolism. Surrealism. Impressionism. Close-ups. Pan-shots. Structure. Spiral. Rotation movement . . . (p. 99)

The expert claims that he has identified the "main axis" of the novel, in a scene taking place in the waiting room of a railway station. The

problem is that while opinions may legitimately vary as to the surrealist content of a literary work, railway stations are rather unmistakable, and the author knows very well that there are none in his
book. Unfortunately, he commits the "stupid blunder" of pointing
out the professor's error, and the two men must endure an excruci-
ating moment.

As enjoyable as these scenes can be, they are not the "main axis"
of Sarraute's book. Indeed, one can, from the passage quoted above,
understand Sartre's complaint: there are doubtless interesting tropisms in this scene between writer and critic, but the prevailing
effect of the paragraph is one of social satire. What Sarraute aims at
is delivered in the eighth section, remarkable in that it is utterly
devoid of the irony that characterizes much of the novel. Here Sarraute intends nothing less than to share with her readers, as much as
possible, the sensation of literary creation:

> There, it seems to him that he senses . . . it is as though there were a sort
> of throb, a pulsation. . . . It stops, starts again, louder, stops once more and
> again starts. . . . It's like the faint, intermittent, persistent sound, the scratch-
> ing, the soft nibbling that signifies to the person who is tensely listening in
> the silence of the night, a living presence. . . .
> It increases, spreads . . . it has the vigor, the untouched freshness of
> young shoots, of new grass, it is growing with the same restrained violence,
> propelling words before it. . . . They attract one another. . . . Their fine jet is
> lengthening. . . . Suddenly the impetus becomes more forceful, it is a brief
> eruption, irresistibly the words come rushing, and then everything grows
> calm. (p. 64)

It is a delicate moment that Sarraute wants to communicate, when
the book hovers between creation and extinction: "it's dead. It's
alive" (p. 69). The American writer Mary McCarthy, in an essay
written in 1969, found that Sarraute had succeeded admirably in
portraying the writing process: "Nothing of the sort—a rending of
the veil—has been attempted before, and one would have said in
advance that it was impossible, short of demonstration, to show
how an author composes. . . . Mme. Sarraute has done it."[9]

Though much of the book can be comic in its focus on the social
aspects of literature, Sarraute's sense of purpose here (and in the
other passage of creation, when the writer begins a new book) is so
striking that the reader understands that the portrayal of the process
of literary creation in this scene, not the satire, is what the book is

meant to convey. Indeed, so impressively is the process of creation treated here that one feels that all the little pomposities, evasions, and fabrications of the writer fade into insignificance next to the writing itself.

Between Life and Death has another dimension that is important for any study of the evolution of Sarraute's writing, namely, an awareness of the nonreferential aspects of language that seemed to some critics more sophisticated than what is found in her earlier books. The novel was published in 1968, when questions of language, or *écriture*, were much discussed in French theoretical circles. The *New* Novel seemed to many the logical place to encounter creative works that shared a common interest with critics and theorists, new texts that coincided with new theories. It is of such a coincidence that Stephen Heath writes, in 1972:

The context in which *Between Life and Death* is to be understood is that shift in the development of the novel form represented by the practice of writing. The situation of this shift . . . is not to be grasped in traditional accounts of a change from Balzacian realism to psychological realism or whatever, but at the level of writing, the practice of which is now the experience of that practice.[10]

The novel, then, does not represent anything outside of itself.

The extreme of this view is that there is no reality outside language, and it can be readily seen that there is a fundamental difficulty in reconciling Sarraute's theory of tropisms and this new view of language: for example, she believes that one cannot communicate tropisms simply by *naming* them, for the name merely provokes a conventionalized response in the reader. The characters who use words freely and dismissively in *Portrait of a Man Unknown* are precisely the *inauthentic* characters, who fail to grasp the real intensity of life beneath their casual labels. Finally, in all her discussions of the detection of tropisms, it is apparent that Sarraute conceives of them as something preverbal: the sensation of psychic activity comes first, remarkable partly *because* it cannot be defined. The writer's task is not to name the tropism, for that would destroy it, but to create, in language of course, evocative images that will cause the reader to experience an analogous emotional stirring (see chapter 2).

To be sure, there does appear in *Between Life and Death* to be an increased awareness of the very considerable role that language must play in all this. Much of Sarraute's description of the creative process does echo structuralist preoccupation with textuality, with *écriture*. When he is a boy, the writer's future vocation announces itself in a fascination with wordplay: "Hérault, héraut, héros, aire haut, erre haut, R.O." (p. 16).[11] The description of the creative process is very intimately involved with words:

[Words] open out, the thread that runs through them grows taut, they are vibrating . . . he listens as their resonance reverberates. . . . Alone with them, he himself completely set right, outside the soft, insipid substance into which he had been plunged, he is delighted with their movements, he places and displaces them, to make them form more skillfully shaped arabesques. Their vibration increases, it has now become music, song, an accentuated march. The rhythms create one another, as though by attraction words arrive from all sides.(p. 65)

Words do indeed function autonomously, obeying their own impulses, but that is something one must guard against:

They play, answer, echo one another. They reverberate. They reflect one another, they sparkle. . . . And he is caught in the labyrinth of their mirrors, imprisoned in the interlacings of their reflections. . . . He turns, mirrored from one to the other. . . .
One must tear oneself away from that, go out in the bright daylight, there where everything is mat and mute . . . relax, rest, forget . . . (p. 67)

Why must one tear oneself away? Because the danger of language is that it will suppress the living substance that exists before language and that is the purpose of writing. The following passage is taken from the last section, when the writer embarks on his second book:

For a long time he examines the image . . . the elegant sobriety, the perfect precision of the sentences. Contained within their outlines the words flow along in a continual stream. . . . And yet something has disappeared . . . a shy impetus, a trembling, he looks for it . . . the thing that like a little blind animal propelled itself, pushing the words before it, he no longer feels it . . . it has been stifled, set in the starchiness of these frozen sentences. . . . Just here, perhaps, there would seem to be a sort of vibration, a pulsation . . . a barely perceptible pulse is beating . . . he will have to hurry before it is too late, if not, he knows now what will happen . . . the fine sentences are going to gather together in a form that one of these days will take on the lugubrious aspect of a field strewn with corpses. (p. 176)

A few years after the publication of *Between Life and Death*, in 1971, a colloquium on the New Novel was held at Cerisy. It was at this time that the term *nouveau nouveau roman* was coined to designate a novelistic form that would keep pace with critical theory. This second phase of the New Novel, as Lois Oppenheim explains, reflects the belief that literature does not refer to things outside it but follows its own internal mechanisms: "[T]his fiction became linked, through the ensemble of theoretical formulations surrounding it, with the antireferential motif that sought to abstract narrative realism from its perceptual ties with the world and to resituate it on the level of mechanical construction."[12] Sarraute, who attended the first day of the conference, reiterated her belief that tropisms exist before language, and are perceived—however faintly—before they are formulated in words: "To say that there is no pre-language, that everything begins with words . . . is absolutely impossible for me."[13] As *Between Life and Death* shows, her attitude toward literary language was never naive, but language for her must always go hand in hand with a tropistic substance that exists first. In 1982, at another colloquium, this time at New York University, she spoke again of the role of language in the pursuit of tropisms: "[A kind of writing] was alive because it brought to the outside something still intact, something which had not already been taken over by language, something still vague, still hazy. In order for it to take shape, it had to be carried by words, to slide into words, to melt with a language from which it would be inseparable."[14]

Can a concept such as the "New Novel" have any currency if it claims writers as different as Robbe-Grillet and Sarraute? It should be understood that this association with the New Novel is not something that Sarraute needs to ensure her reputation, nor is it something that she herself stressed, especially after the concerns of the "New New Novel" began to be articulated. Robbe-Grillet was an enthusiastic participant in those formulations, while Sarraute was content to leave a widening gulf between herself and Robbe-Grillet's circle. But even before that, when she wrote a preface for the 1962 edition of *The Age of Suspicion*, she used the occasion to discuss the evolution of her own work, without reference to that of her contemporaries. She concludes, almost as though she were reluctant to make such a claim, "It goes without saying that most of the ideas expressed in these articles constitute certain of the fundamental notions of what is called today the 'New Novel.'"[15] This rather weak claim invites one to question the validity of the term "New Novel."

One point the two writers certainly have in common is the desire, at which they arrived independently, to be *new*. Moreover, there are common features in their attitudes toward the recent history of the novel: both cite as predecessors the modernist writers: Proust, Kafka, Joyce, Dostoevsky, Flaubert, with Sarraute favoring the more psychological writers in this group (Proust, Joyce, and Dostoevsky), Robbe-Grillet favoring the behaviorist side (Kafka, for example). The "old" novel for both of them is nineteenth-century realist fiction, which both find to be admired excessively by their contemporaries. One might add that Sarraute's account of this continuing admiration is fuller than Robbe-Grillet's; to read *For a New Novel*, one would think that French critics and academics of the 1950s had never heard of the modernist novel, except perhaps for Proust, whom they contrived to treat as a special kind of realist. Sarraute does a better job of explaining their attitude: the modernist experiment in fiction had produced interesting results, but was essentially ended, whereas the realist novel as Balzac defined it was timeless. In either case, however, the two agreed that it was high time that the novel change.

Beyond this very general point of agreement, one encounters the fact that the two writers' theories are quite different; Robbe-Grillet rejects psychological depths for surfaces, whereas Sarraute wants to probe those depths further than had been done before. But *For a New Novel* does not represent Robbe-Grillet's fictional practice very well, and as it happens, the resulting myth about Robbe-Grillet—that he rejects all subjectivity and psychology—is precisely the point that separates him most from Sarraute. If one considers his novelistic practice and Sarraute's, there is indeed some common ground.

When one ignores the myth of a purely *chosiste* Robbe-Grillet, it is clear that much of his work is an attempt to *make problematic* the pursuit of meaning rather than to eliminate it. There is, then, a clear parallel between his work and Sarraute's. In *Portrait of a Man Unknown*, tropisms stand as a refutation of the usual, cut-and-dried mode of understanding the world and human relationships. Sarraute's narrator, groping for a new vision of human psychology, is thus in some respects like Robbe-Grillet's detectives: he is seeking meaning in a situation that questions entire modes of understanding. In that respect, both novelists have connections to existential phenomenology. Sarraute's narrator in *Portrait of a Man Unknown* perceives psychological relationships in a new way that is not available to those who cannot or will not go beyond the traditional framework within which one discusses relationships and personality. Doubtless the priorities of the two are different: Robbe-Grillet questions the intelligibility of the world in a more general way than Sarraute. For him, any framework in which one claims to find straightforward meaning is suspect, whereas Sarraute's interest is more specifically in a new view of psychology. But a similarity arises in their common need to refute traditional modes of perception, and it is much more defensible to call them both New Novelists than it would appear from a discussion of their theoretical essays alone.

5

Michel Butor

Of all the New Novelists, Michel Butor has had perhaps the most multifaceted involvement in the world of letters. He began writing poetry while still in school, and as a young man associated with surrealist writers and painters, including André Breton, the onetime leader of the movement. He pursued a degree in philosophy and had a long teaching career, including university appointments in France, England, the United States, and Switzerland.

He began to write fiction in the 1950s, during the time when the concept of the New Novel was being formulated. His first four novels, *Passage de Milan* (1954), *L'Emploi du temps* (*Passing Time;* 1956), *La Modification* (*A Change of Heart;* 1957), and *Degrés* (*Degrees;* 1960), are sometimes referred to as his New Novel period, or simply as his novel period. After 1960, he essentially abandoned the novel, turning to new and different forms. *Mobile* (1962) is subtitled "Study for a Representation of the United States"; *6.810.000 litres d'eau par seconde* (*Niagara;* 1965) is a "stereophonic study," and *Portrait de l'artiste en jeune singe* (*Portrait of the Artist as a Young Ape;* 1967) is called by the author a "cappricio."

Essays on the Novel

Butor is often called the most cerebral of the New Novelists: he studied with the philosophers Gaston Bachelard and Maurice Merleau-Ponty and considered his turn to the novel an attempt to unite philosophy and poetry.[1] He has also published a great deal of literary criticism. For these reasons, his ideas about the novel seem less monolithic than those of some of the other New Novelists, less a "theory of the novel" than observations about the genre within the context of a larger and more diversified body of work. His first volume of collected essays, *Répertoire* (*Inventory;* 1960), covers a wide range of topics. Some of his essays on the novel, first collected in *Inventory*, were subsequently published in *Essais sur le roman* (*Essays on the Novel*), but the volume is not quite the same sort of work as

Robbe-Grillet's *For a New Novel* or Sarraute's *The Age of Suspicion:* it does not pursue a single line of argument as much as the other two do, and it was not published until 1969, which is rather too late to be a defining moment in the history of the New Novel. Moreover, the volume does not contain all of Butor's most important essays on fiction.

Nevertheless, one can identify in Butor's work certain ideas regarding the novel that are sufficient to relate his thought to that of the other New Novelists. Like them, Butor felt that the novel was at an important juncture in its history, and like them, he advocated a "new" novel in relation to the traditional realist fiction of the nineteenth century—although there is in Butor a subtler attitude toward the traditional novel, as will be shown presently.

Butor considered the novel in its relationship to culture as a whole, as one of the many narratives that combine to form what he has called the "mythology" of a culture, others being, for example, history, the educational system, the press, even casual conversation among family or friends.[2] Together these narratives constitute the filter through which one perceives the world, the means by which one organizes what is commonly called reality. The novel, then, as well as these other narratives, may be considered to present a perspective on reality; there is no firm boundary between the real and the imaginary. One can see in these ideas the influence of Butor's study of phenomenology; indeed, he calls the novel "the phenomenological realm par excellence" (p. 27).[3] Other narratives that help constitute reality, such as history or dinner-table conversation about the events of the day, are at least in principle verifiable by appealing to information from a different source; the novel, however, is unverifiable and must rely on its own internal mechanisms to convince the reader. In this respect the novel resembles the phenomenological understanding of consciousness; phenomenology brackets beliefs concerning the external existence of the objects of consciousness, dealing instead with the act of consciousness itself.

An artist's research into and experimentation with the mechanisms of fiction, Butor believed, thus are intimately connected with our understanding of the world. First, awareness of the many technical possibilities available to fiction will cure one of the misapprehension that the traditional novel is the natural or universal way to tell stories. The traditional novel will then be seen in relation to cultural mythology, "that fundamental narrative in which our whole life is steeped" (p. 28).

Butor also believed that one can study the "real" by studying the novel, and a constant theme in his writing about narrative is the revelations that may be had by working on aspects of fiction that are seemingly only of formal interest. For example, if one attempts to follow a strict chronological order in a narrative, relating events only as they are supposed to happen, without flashbacks, a whole view of the characters is imposed: "all reference to universal history becomes impossible, all reference to the past of the characters encountered, to memory, and consequently all interiority. Thus the characters are necessarily transformed into things. They are visible only from the outside, and it is almost impossible, in fact, to make them talk" (p. 18). Thus one can see that the seemingly simple process of inserting events into a chronology implies and entails a particular view of human existence.

Finally, the novel is a means of integrating one's experience in a changing modern world. To insist on unchanging, traditional forms of fiction leaves one without the conceptual tools required to organize the vast flow of new information that characterizes life in the modern world: "Now, it is clear that the world in which we live is being transformed with great rapidity. Traditional narrative techniques are incapable of integrating all the new relations thus created. There results a perpetual uneasiness; it is impossible for our consciousness to organize all the information that assails it" (p. 28). Thus the novel, from the point of view not only of the novelist but also of the reader, becomes nothing less than a way of living.

Butor's attitude toward the traditional novel has similarities to both Robbe-Grillet's and Sarraute's. He shares with Robbe-Grillet the conviction that form and content cannot be separated, that a particular technique implies a certain world view. But he also thinks, like Sarraute, that one of the worst effects of the traditional novel is that it has become so familiar that everyone merely takes it for granted, conventional techniques generating conventionalized responses. The exploration of reality that the novel should be cannot take place if all one explores is a well-beaten path:

The novelist who refuses to accept this task, never discarding old habits, never demanding any particular effort of his reader, never obliging him to confront himself, to question attitudes long since taken for granted, will

certainly enjoy a readier success, but he becomes the accomplice of that
profound uneasiness, that darkness, in which we are groping for our way.
He stiffens the reflexes of our consciousness even more, making any
awakening more difficult; he contributes to its suffocation, so that even if
his intentions are more generous, his work is in the last analysis a poison.
(p. 28)

Butor often argues that what he wants for the novel is a more
advanced "realism." He uses this term perhaps because in the
polemic climate of the 1950s and 1960s, the New Novel was so often
attacked for being unrealistic, and many practitioners were compelled to defend themselves in the terms used in the attack. But by
"realism" he does not mean a fiction that would straightforwardly
represent an objective reality outside the limits of the fiction itself,
for there can be no such thing. Rather, he argues for a novel that is
realistic in the sense that it is profoundly linked with our percep-
tions of reality, and it is clear to Butor that this kind of realism leads
to techniques quite unlike those of the realist fiction of the nineteenth century. Since the link between fiction and reality is best seen
when its functioning is made explicit by exploration of its various
alternative forms, "the novel tends naturally toward its own eluci-
dation" (p. 30). The novel is, then, inherently reflexive. The traditional novel tends not to explore its own mechanisms because it
dare not; it depends for its very being on the illusion that it
describes something outside itself. To lift the veil would bring
destruction: "those forms . . . could not be reflected upon without
immediately revealing their inadequacy, their untruthfulness[;]
those forms . . . give us an image of reality in flagrant contradiction
to the reality which gave them birth and which they are concerned
to pass over in silence" (p. 30). Thus self-conscious fiction, far from
being the frivolous, unrealistic kind of play that realists see in it,
possesses high moral seriousness: "[nonreflexive, realist novels] are
impostures which it is the duty of criticism to expose; for such
works, for all their charms and merits, preserve and deepen the
darkness, imprison consciousness in its contradictions, in its blind-
ness, which risks leading it into the most fatal disorders" (p. 30).

Refreshingly, Butor is one New Novelist willing to speak posi-
tively of the accomplishments of the novelist so often represented to
be the quintessence of traditional fiction, Honoré de Balzac. He sees
better than many other participants in the New Novel debate—on
both sides—that the traditional Balzac is largely a figment of the

imagination. Indeed, if it is sometimes difficult to find a Balzac novel that answers the description drawn up by Balzac's detractors (and even his defenders), Butor explains that it is because the concept of the Balzacian novel is drawn from only a tiny part of Balzac's production.[4]

La Comédie humaine (*The Human Comedy*), published between 1842 and 1848, is the name Balzac gave to a collected edition of his novels and stories. Perhaps because many of the novels were written years before Balzac had the idea of this grand scheme, many readers continue to read the novels as separate works, noting no more in the way of unity than the fact that several characters occur in more than one tale. Butor argues that while one can demonstrate that a work such as *Eugénie Grandet*, considered in isolation, can be shown to be old-fashioned, if one takes *The Human Comedy* as a whole, then Balzac's work gains in richness and is much closer to the preoccupations of the mid twentieth century, such as the instability of reality and the importance of perspective.

This argument is not the same as the one advanced by both Robbe-Grillet and Sarraute, that Balzac was the New Novelist of the 1830s in the sense that techniques that are now familiar were innovative at the time. Butor does include some interesting material showing Balzac to be self-consciously an innovator (a "new novelist") by deliberately departing from the art of the novel as practiced by Walter Scott, but his main argument is different. Butor's view is that *The Human Comedy* responds to the interests of modern readers and novelists, that Balzac's true inheritors are Proust and Faulkner, not those who profess to follow the Balzacian tradition by writing realist fiction a hundred years after Balzac's death. Butor's argument is interesting primarily for what it says about Butor: it is especially interesting to see what he thinks is modern about Balzac.

By linking together several novels under the rubric *The Human Comedy*, Balzac attains, in Butor's estimation, a mobility of structure that is difficult to create in a single work. Considering *The Human Comedy* as a novel, each reader will read the "chapters" in a different order; indeed, it is impossible to establish a chronology that would account for every event in the work, so there can be no preferred order in which to read the separate parts. Since the reader's understanding of a given story is affected by the oblique illumination provided by related tales, each component novel will in effect be different according to what other stories the reader has read previously. The whole of *The Human Comedy*, then, is a vast, changing reality that must be approached from different points of view. As in the case of the mobile, an object for which Butor has a particular fascination, due to the constant change in the relationship of its delicately balanced parts, what one sees will depend on one's angle of vision.

Balzac's novel also gives Butor a model for the relationship he sees between culture, reality, and narrative. A historical novelist, Balzac includes historical figures in his cast of characters. Such characters have, of course, an objective existence outside the novel, and the novelist is not free to decide, for example, to have Napoleon die at the Battle of Waterloo. At the other extreme, for characters who play relatively obscure roles in the history that the novel purports to describe, Balzac has a free hand: if he needs a messenger to bring Napoleon a dispatch, he can invent one on the spot. A third class of characters is the fictitious famous character: if Balzac wants a famous poet, he might avoid the real Lamartine because of the constraints imposed by the use of historical personalities, but he can invent a fictional Canalis and, if he wants to, make him Lamartine's double in a roman à clef relationship. These different realities become interesting when one shifts from one level to another: a fictional character who appears in a best-selling novel can become more celebrated than the real person on whom he is based, and in later editions of *The Human Comedy*, Balzac replaces references to Lamartine with the name Canalis. Legend has it that Balzac felt his characters' celebrity as acutely as his readers did: on his deathbed, he called for Dr. Bianchon, one of his fictional characters.

Thus Balzac's novel demonstrates the instability of these shifting levels of reality, making problematic the very notion of reality or "working on" reality, as Butor would put it. They also illustrate his idea of the multiple narratives that constitute cultural mythology. In a single Balzac novel, the historical characters refer the reader to the narratives of the real world: history, journalism, political discourse. Imaginary characters refer to other novels in which they occur, and doubles such as Canalis refer to their real models, who themselves stand for a particular class of human being, the way Lamartine represents poets in general. Far from the unequivocal, stable reality of the fictitious "traditional" Balzacian novel, *The Human Comedy* is "a kind of plowing-up, a turning of the soil, a revolution of the image of reality" (p. 113).

What Butor has done with these arguments is turn Balzac into something of a modernist. One of the distinctions between modernist and realist fiction is that the realist novel describes a stable, knowable and known reality, whereas the modernist writer conceives of reality as something that varies from one person to the next, according to experience. The multifaceted reality that Butor finds in *The Human Comedy* must be approached from a point of view: there is no privileged perspective from which the world can be seen objectively.

A Change of Heart (1957)

With his first two novels, Butor got off to a slow start, but with *A Change of Heart* he produced a bona fide bestseller. The book won the Renaudot prize, and 100,000 copies of the first edition were sold. By 1986, total sales approached half a million copies. Two factors are often cited in explanation of the book's success: first, it is said to be one of the most accessible of the New Novels; second, the book appears superficially to endorse bourgeois morality. In fact, neither of these assertions holds up very well under close scrutiny.

The novel relates the journey by train of Léon Delmont, the head of the Paris office of the Italian typewriter manufacturer Scabelli, from Paris to Rome. It is a trip he often makes for business reasons, but this time he is going to Rome to tell his mistress, Cécile, the happy news that he has found her a job in Paris, and that he plans to leave his wife, Henriette, to live with her. During the course of the trip, however, he comes to realize that his feelings for Cécile are inseparable from his love of Rome, and that his dream of moving her to Paris is at bottom the impossible desire to transplant Rome itself to France. By journey's end he has changed his mind and decided to stay with Henriette. As an attempt to salvage something from the experience, he will write a novel about this episode in his life.

In terms of technical innovation, Butor chose a device that has attracted a good deal of critical discussion but that does not interfere greatly with the casual reader's processing of the text: the story is told in the second person (in French, in the polite *vous* as opposed to the familiar *tu*). The novel begins this way: "Standing with your left foot on the grooved brass sill, you try in vain with your right shoulder to push the sliding door a little wider open."[5] The device has been interpreted in a number of ways: some commentators see it as a means of promoting reader identification; others find different effects, including that of *distancing* the reader from the story. Butor's explanation is found in an essay on "The Use of Personal Pronouns in the Novel."[6] Reviewing more familiar narrative discourses, Butor argues that the third-person narrative relates the story as though the identity of the observer were of no consequence because what is being said is not a matter of individual perspective; the use of the first person supposes, on the other hand, that the observer's point of view is important because the truth is relative to his or her perspective. The second person, he goes on to say, is useful for a situation in which a character's understanding of his or her own story is at first imperfect: the narrative voice that addresses Léon Delmont says things about him that he does not yet know himself, at least not on the level of language. By using the second person, Butor can bring his character to self-awareness and eventually to the active use of his own voice, in the novel that Delmont decides to write at the end of *A Change of Heart*.

The psychological insights alone are sufficient to sustain the reader's interest. Reviewing his plan to leave his wife, Delmont shows himself capable of remarkable self-deception by reflecting that he will thus provide his four children with the example of a man with sufficient courage to obey the dictates of his heart (p. 65). His feeling at age 45 of being trapped in a stale marriage is conventional enough but is made more interesting by his suspicion that what Henriette feels for him is primarily contempt rather than some more predictable emotion. When Cécile comes to Paris on holiday, Delmont invites her to dinner to meet Henriette, introducing her as a Roman acquaintance. He vaguely intends thereby to soften the blow that must inevitably fall on Henriette, but to his dismay the two women get along famously, even seeming to unite against him: whereas Delmont has always portrayed Henriette as a religious bigot to the virulently anti-Catholic Cécile, Cécile's impression is very different: "She's far more broad-minded than you, and you can stop deluding yourself—you're no longer all-important to her" (p. 161).

But *A Change of Heart* gains infinitely in interest when one turns away from the plot to questions of symbolism and structure. Moreover, when one pays close attention to these highly complex matters, the moral lessons of the book—and moral lessons there are—are seen to be quite different from the straightforward praise of bourgeois marital fidelity.

Beginning with the book's setting, one can see that Butor took pains to establish a certain structure and to ensure that the reader pay attention to it. Each of the nine chapters begins with Delmont entering his third-class railway compartment and ends with him leaving it, reserving his place with a book bought in the Paris station. In other words, everything transpiring outside the compartment, Delmont's actions in the world and its actions on him, must first come into the compartment before the reader can learn about it. The situation is very like that of the human consciousness from the phenomenological point of view: what one focuses on is not the objective reality of the outside world but the perception of that reality through acts of consciousness. The exterior scenes that Delmont sees through the window, such as passing stations and other landmarks, are primarily stimuli to his thoughts, to the main activity occurring inside the train. In this compartment, Delmont reflects on the past, present, and future; *A Change of Heart* is, as Mary Lydon puts it, a "train of thought."[7]

This thought is highly introspective; it is an exploration and reevaluation of Delmont's self and its relationship with the outside world. One of the many cultural images that inform the book is the ancient French legend of the Great Huntsman, a ghostlike horseman associated with the Forest of Fontainebleau (and other places). As Delmont's train passes Fontainebleau, his imagination dwells on this legendary figure and on the question with which the Great Huntsman accosts passersby: "Can you hear me?" (p. 95). Throughout the rest of the book, the phantom reappears several times, asking different questions; taken together, these questions indicate that the Great Huntsman is an externalization of Delmont's anguished self-examination: "What are you waiting for?" (p. 114), "Where are you?" (p, 128), "Are you mad?" (p. 156), and finally, "Who are you?" (p. 181).

The action of the book lasts the duration of the journey from Paris to Rome, something less than 24 hours. But the simplicity of this framework—a short span of time, an uncomplicated journey from one city to another, a compact and sharply delineated setting—is deceptive. Delmont's thought has a mobility far more complex than the linear, unidirectional movement of the train. In his compartment, he recalls not only scenes from his life with Henriette and with Cécile but also several other train trips between Paris and Rome: the routine business trip to Rome the week before this one, another trip to Rome when he first met Cécile, his trip with Cécile to Paris and their return to Rome, two trips to Rome with Henriette, the first being their honeymoon before the war, and even a future trip, his return to Paris from the present visit. The narrative switches from one trip to another without overt transitions, although without the wrenching dislocations that Robbe-Grillet produces in *Jealousy:* if the reader ever gets lost in these changes, it is only for a short time. Nevertheless, Butor is able to make his point that the linear chronology with which we are accustomed to arrange human experience has almost no bearing on the way we subjectively perceive our experience.

In keeping with Butor's ideas about cultural mythology and about the perception of reality, Delmont's consciousness operates against an extraordinarily rich cultural background. The desires and fears with which he struggles during this period of introspection are aligned along three related axes: Paris-Rome, modern-ancient, and Catholic-pagan. One can gain some idea of the depth of cultural information with which Butor informs his story by analyzing the significance of Delmont's Paris address, 15 Place du Panthéon. The Parisian monument (which Delmont can see from his apartment) is a Roman presence in Paris. It unites two eras as well, first because it is a modern (1764–1789) edifice with an ancient counterpart and also because the Roman Pantheon is the best-preserved of the city's ancient buildings. Both the Roman and Parisian Pantheons have had changing religious significations as well. As its name suggests, the Roman version was constructed as a temple to all the pagan gods; the building escaped destruction because Boniface IV transformed it in 609 into a church dedicated to Mary. The Parisian Panthéon is today a national mausoleum but was first built as the church of Sainte-Geneviève, the patron saint of Paris. With his particular obsessions, Léon Delmont could have no other address.

The associations of Rome in Delmont's mind are multiple, and getting to the bottom of them is what *A Change of Heart* is really about. On one level, since Cécile lives in Rome, the city represents love, youth, and another chance at happiness for him, in contrast to Paris, where Henriette has just insisted that the family stage a rather grim celebration of Delmont's 45th birthday. Rome is characterized by sunshine and the simple pleasures of life as well. In one scene, on his return to Paris from the usual business trip to Rome, he tries to prolong his contact with Italy by taking lunch in an Italian restaurant instead of eating at home with Henriette as usual. But to no avail: the spaghetti Bolognese is unsatisfactory, the promised espresso turns out to be a *filtre*, and when he emerges from the restaurant, the Parisian rain extinguishes his last Italian cigarette (p. 58). Lucid enough to know that it may be his mood, not the restaurant, that spoiled his lunch, Delmont also knows that it makes no difference: Paris for him is indelibly marked with drabness.

But Léon Delmont is also a man of culture, and it is the associations of high culture that are the most important: rather than being a backdrop for a love story, the art of Rome is essential to Delmont's introspection. Most of his time with Cécile is spent touring the city, with a substantial focus on art. Indeed, this aspect of their relationship is apparent from the beginning: he meets Cécile on the train to Rome (she is returning from a vacation in Paris), spends the balance of the trip with her, accompanies her to her apartment, leaves without even learning her name, but somehow he knows that they will meet again, get to know each other, and "soon she'd admit you not only into that tall Roman house into which she'd disappeared but also into the whole of her district, *into a whole section of Rome that was still unknown to you*" (p. 92; my italics). Once they become lovers, they explore the city in depth, devoting weekends to studies of Borromini and Caravaggio, for example (p. 141). Rome is an integral part of their relationship: "and when you walked about the Forum together, you were not only surrounded by the few forlorn stones, the broken capitals, the impressive brick walls or foundations; you were in the midst of a vast shared dream which grew more solid, more detailed and more authentic with every visit" (pp. 141–42).

There is one place they cannot go, however: the anti-Catholic Cécile refuses to set foot in the Vatican. When one day Delmont notes that their itineraries have never included Michelangelo, Cécile immediately accuses him of trying to trick her into visiting the Sistine Chapel: "In spite of all your protests, you're really corrupted to the core with Christianity" (p. 142).

For it is quite true that although Delmont "hates popes and priests" and intends his separation from Henriette to be a break from "all that harness of vain scruples" (pp. 46, 30), his obsession with Rome is inextricably bound up with Christianity. It is not only that so much art in Rome is Christian; Cécile's remark has some foundation. When Delmont thinks to himself that he ought to visit (without Cécile, of course) all the churches dedicated to Saint

Agnes, then all the Saint Giovannis, and so on, it is in order to make "strange discoveries about the Christian world, which is itself so wrongly understood" (p. 142), and he recognizes that it is with some justification that Cécile believes that the Vatican represents what has been keeping him from leaving Henriette (pp. 79–80). Cécile's characterization of Delmont as "corrupted to the core" is partisan and emotional; put more objectively, one can see that Butor's point here is that Catholicism, too, is part of Delmont's cultural background and has left its imprint on his perception of reality.

The tension between pagan and Christian Rome reaches a crisis in Delmont's fitful and sporadic dreaming during the night portion of the voyage. The most important cultural referents in the dream are Virgil's *Aeneid*, particularly Book VI, in which Aeneas consults the Sibyl and visits the underworld, and Michelangelo's *The Last Judgment*, in the Sistine Chapel. Both these works are linked to both pagan and Christian Rome. Virgil predates Christianity, of course, but "was considered throughout the Middle Ages as the epitome of that within imperial Rome which made Christian Rome possible, as the 'pagan prophet.' "[8] Michelangelo as artist combined classical form and Christian belief, and in his dream Delmont sees *The Last Judgment*, in which the pagan sibyls are grouped with the Old Testament prophets.

In the *Aeneid*, the Sibyl provides Aeneas with the Golden Bough to guide him through the underworld, but Delmont's Sibyl refuses his request for the same on the grounds of insufficient self-awareness: "No, not for you, not for those who know their own desires so ill; you'll have to trust to the wavering light that will appear when this poor fire of mine is out" (p. 185). The light is perhaps an allusion to the dim blue light that is the only illumination in the train compartment during the nighttime hours, and which may represent the spark of Delmont's introspective consciousness. Delmont-Aeneas dreams of being ferried across the river Styx by a blend of the classical boatman Charon and the Great Huntsman: "What are you waiting for? Can you hear me? Who are you? I have come to take you to the farther bank. I can see that you are dead; have no fear of capsizing, your weight will not sink the boat" (p. 189).

Aeneas finds the spirit of his father, Anchises, in the Elysian Fields, but Delmont ends up encountering his spiritual father, the pope, and a procession of cardinals. These figures, appearing near the end of Delmont's dream and near the end of his journey, begin

to make explicit the contradiction in himself that Delmont is beginning to understand. The cardinals whisper to him, "Why do you
profess to hate us? Are we not Romans?" (p. 225), and the pope
addresses him in these terms:

> O you who lie paralyzed in mid-air at my feet, unable to move your lips
> or even to close your eyes to escape my apparition,
> you who long to sleep, and to feel beneath you the solid ground which is
> now denied you,
> watched over by so many images which you can neither set in order nor
> identify,
> why do you profess to love Rome? Am I not the ghost of the emperors,
> haunting, through the ages, the capital of their lost and longed-for world?
> (p. 225)

Arriving in Rome, and fully awake, Delmont now realizes why he
has been so obsessed with Rome, his "lost and longed-for world."
Cécile is only a symptom of his real need, which has to do more
with philosophy and history than with love: "You were trying to
counterbalance your dissatisfaction with Paris by a secret belief in a
return to the Pax Romana, a world empire organized around a capi-
tal city which might perhaps not be Rome but, for example, Paris"
(p. 243). It is the "mythos of Rome itself" that has been driving him
(p. 243), the need for an ordered world, nostalgia for a bygone era:

> And thus you are aware that one of the great epochs of history has come to
> an end, that in which the world had a center, which was not only the earth
> set amidst the spheres, in the Ptolemaic system, but was Rome in the center
> of the earth. (p. 243)

The memory of the Empire, which dominated all the dreams of
Europe for so many centuries, is now no longer an adequate image
to represent the future of the world, which for each one of us has
become far vaster and differently organized. And that was why,
when you tried to make closer contact with it on your own account,
the image fell to pieces (p. 243).

With this view of history in mind, the role of Catholicism in *A
Change of Heart* can be seen in a new light. The self-aware, thus
improved, Delmont of the end of the novel knows that he will go
back to Henriette, and it is indeed partly Catholic scruples that lead

him away from Cécile. But while the book may recognize the weight
of cultural and religious training, it does not at all make an overall
endorsement of Catholicism. Rather, the Church, centered in Rome
and led by the Holy Father, must be seen as another inadequate
image of the modern world. Delmont is attracted to the Church by
his training and by the beauty of its art but on the most profound
level by the false promise of an ordered world. This religious order
is another image that falls to pieces when approached; the pope is
indeed the "ghost of the emperors."

Butor's glancing reference to another modern imitation of the
order of the ancient world makes it clear that he does not admire or
advocate such bogus attempts to reconstruct the missing center.
During his prewar honeymoon trip to Rome with Henriette, the
pleasure Delmont takes in the city is unspoiled by his knowledge
that Mussolini's Fascists are in power: "Everything seemed mar-
velous to you, uniforms and *'Viva il Duce'* notwithstanding" (p. 232).

Delmont's new understanding does not bring a solution to the
"fissure in my being" (p. 240), for the gap that he has discovered
within him is connected with history itself. He makes a mental
promise to Henriette at the end of the book: "[W]e'll come back to
Rome together, as soon as the waves of this perturbation have died
down, as soon as you've forgiven me; we won't be so very old"
(p. 248). This promise might be taken as an optimistic sign that Delmont has learned to appreciate the real joys of bourgeois family
values, but Vivian Mercier argues persuasively against such a reading by noting that the point has been made throughout the book
that Delmont *is* old; Charon can tell at a glance that he is dead. And
by finally seeing through his illusions, he has if anything grown
older.[9]

Salvation will be sought on a different front altogether: "I ought
to write a book; that would be the way to fill this hollow emptiness
within me, now that I've lost all other freedom" (p. 238). The book
will bring to its readers the awareness that Delmont has come to; it
will "show the part Rome can play in the life of a man in Paris"
(p. 243). While the book will not itself try to revive Delmont's illusions—it will "maintain the distance between these two cities"—it
will also show the "points of contact" between Rome and Paris, and
Cécile will perhaps be able to forgive him when she reads a book in
which "she would appear in her full beauty, adorned with the glory
of Rome" (p. 246).

In an interview published in 1960, Butor suggests that Delmont's salvation will come from a quality that critics recognize in Butor himself: didacticism. Butor's conception of the novel's relationship to reality is key:

Destined to disappear, Léon saves himself through the work of art. If for him there is no way out, that is not necessarily so for everyone, and others, his children, will be less condemned because he has shown them why he is. He will put his entire life in the service of a transformation of reality that he himself will not witness; but he can benefit from it—by his certainty that everything he is doing leads in a certain direction.[10]

If *A Change of Heart* is one of the most accessible of the New Novels, it is also one that has rather obvious connections to an earlier novelistic tradition: in many respects, *A Change of Heart* is a modernist novel. There are of course many definitions of the modernist tradition in fiction, but common to most is the idea that the modernist sees a collapsed order in the world and believes that if order can be recovered, it is only on the individual level and, very often, in the work of art. This element of modernism would not be a bad summary of *A Change of Heart*. Moreover, the modernist novel focuses on individual consciousness rather than on collectivity and often shows that consciousness in the act of self-examination. There is a marked predilection for the theme of the voyage, with such representatives as Conrad's *Heart of Darkness*, Gide's *The Immoralist*, and Mann's *Death in Venice;* these modernist voyages lead to *inner* epiphanies. The modernist novel in contrast to realism tends to avoid closure; there is an unfinished aspect to the end of the story— in this case, Léon Delmont's somewhat tentative plan to write a book. All of these points are essential to any discussion of *A Change of Heart*, even if one approaches the book in isolation, making no attempt to relate it to any other literary movement. The modernist aspects of Butor's novel are fundamental, not incidental.

Niagara (1965)

If a novel such as *A Change of Heart* does not make a great many radical formal innovations, one should nevertheless not think that Butor among the New Novelists is comparatively uninterested in exploring literature's technical possibilities. Quite to the contrary, the phase of his work beginning after the novel *Degrees* (1962) is innovative to the point that one is unsure how to classify such works as *Mobile* (1962) and *Niagara*, which abandon plot and narrative. One critic calls this Butor's second "novelistic" period;[11] others see this development in Butor's career as the abandonment of the novel form altogether.

Niagara and *Mobile* are two of Butor's American texts: *Mobile* has 50 chapters, one devoted to each state of the union, and *Niagara* takes Niagara Falls as its focus. At the same time, they are creative works that reflect some of Butor's most wide-ranging theoretical interests.

In an essay entitled "The Book as Object," Butor seeks to identify and to question the role of the book as opposed to other methods, both historical and contemporary, of recording speech.[12] He concludes that the book's uniqueness is that it is not just a purely sequential record of speech, as is an audio tape, a film, or an ancient scroll. The book has a third dimension, depth; we call a book a *volume* (p. 41). The reader is not required always to read from beginning to end: a book can be leafed through; it is physically possible to read a book in any order, or in different orders. What with the mass distribution of books and the culture of consumption, modern readers have forgotten this special feature. Many go through one paperback book after another; in an earlier age, when a book was owned and used for life, readers were more likely to understand that one of a book's prime functions was to afford them a fundamental *mobility*.

From this (re)discovery, Butor proceeds to a discussion of other of the book's resources. He is in this discussion much influenced by the poet Mallarmé, whose work *Un coup de dés* (1897) makes use of the typographical arrangement of words on the page, different typefaces, and blank spaces. Throughout this essay, Butor attempts to discover new possibilities. In his discussion of enumeration in such works as Rabelais's *Gargantua* and the Bible, he points out that lists can bring words and concepts into unexpected proximity and create relations among them: alphabetical order is a supposedly neutral ordering principle, but each of us remembers an incident in which the position of our name in an alphabetical list played a significant role (p. 47).

Niagara makes extensive use of these and other possibilities. The work was intended as a radio broadcast, which at first seems to contradict the virtues of mobility, since a listener ordinarily must submit to the sequential delivery of the text. But in an oblique way, the limitations of the medium actually serve to underscore the concepts that interest Butor. First, he establishes 10 tracks from which the broadcaster can choose, each a combination of different sections of the text. Moreover, the work makes use of what was in 1965 fairly new technology: it is intended to be broadcast stereophonically, the different voices emanating from the right or left channel, or the center, or moving from left to right. Moreover, the listener is invited to manipulate the channel-balance controls of the receiver to highlight one portion or another of the text. Finally, in the printed text of the same work, the reader is invited to choose which portions to read in a way that at first seems merely practical: "Busy readers will take the short track by skipping all the parentheses and all the preludes."[13] But then Butor adds, after inviting leisurely readers to read everything,

But all the readers of this book will enjoy following the directions for the use of the parentheses and exploring little by little the eight intermediate tracks in order to hear how, within this liquid monument, a change in lighting will cause new forms and aspects to appear. (p. 2)

Butor concludes the section of the book in which he explains where in the radio broadcast the different voices and other sound effects will be heard with a remark specifically aimed at the reader: "Since the mobility of reading is much greater than that of any listening, you may imagine, with book in hand, all kinds of combinations" (p. 13). Although every reader in the world has no doubt had the experience of skipping about in a book, being *told* by the author to omit certain parts is unsettling, which is probably the very feeling Butor intended. The titles *Mobile* and *Niagara* themselves are emblems of mobility that have an unsettling effect on conventional opinion: a mobile is a sculpture that changes shape, an image that recalls Heraclitus illustrating his idea that all matter in the universe is constantly changing by observing that one cannot step twice into the same river.[14]

Niagara's text is arranged typographically according to the speakers and the channels through which their voices are heard. In the center, the voices belong to an announcer, who describes the scene, and a reader, who reads descriptions of Niagara Falls from Chateaubriand's

Essai sur les révolutions (1797), *Atala* (1801), and *Mémoires d'outre-tombe* (1849–1850). Speaking from the left and right are a number of couples—newlyweds, and older men and women—and a few single persons. In keeping with Butor's custom of following precise structuring devices in his texts, the couples appear in alphabetical order: Abel and Betty, Charles and Diana (!), Elias and Fanny. The lines spoken by these speakers are interleaved, so that reading down the page line by line, for example, one might read first a fragment of a sentence by the announcer, then a bit of Chateaubriand text, then a pair of lines spoken by Betty and Abel. Speech that emanates from the left channel is set to the left of the page; left margins of increasing size indicate center-channel and right-channel speech. The voice of the announcer is set in boldface to indicate that it is louder than that of the reader, whose text is set in italics. There are 12 chapters according to the 12 months of the year, starting in April and ending in March. Within each chapter there are subsections called Parentheses and Preludes. The 10 "tracks" are created by reading or omitting various sections and even reading or omitting certain voices in a given section.

Chateaubriand's choice of texts is highly significant. In a long essay on "Chateaubriand and Early America," Butor describes a writer divided between the Christianity he wrote of in *Le Génie du christianisme* (1802) and the powerful forces he discovered in his travels in the American wilderness in 1791.[15] The power of American nature, represented by Niagara Falls, was for Chateaubriand highly charged with eroticism, as may be seen in the following excerpt that Butor uses in *Niagara:*

The mass of the river, which hurls itself southward, bulges and becomes rounded like a vast cylinder at the point of leaving the shore, then unrolls in a sheet of snow and glistens in the sun with all the colors of the prism; the one falling toward the north descends in fearful darkness like a pillar of water from the flood. Countless rainbows curve and cross above the abyss, whose dreadful booming can be heard for sixty miles around. The waters, striking the shaken rock, splash back up in whirlwinds of foam which, rising above trees, resemble the thick smoke of a vast forest fire. Gigantic, immeasurable rocks, cut into phantom forms, adorn the wild scene; wild walnut trees, reddish a scaly with sap-wood, grow, stunted, on these fossil skeletons. (p. 6)

The Native Americans that Chateaubriand encountered seemed to him, unlike Europeans and the European residents of America, to be in harmony with nature—with the external nature in which they lived and with their bodies, with themselves as natural beings (p. 79). One of the texts that Chateaubriand drew from his trip to America was *René* (1802), the story of a young Frenchman who exiles himself among the Natchez of Louisiana. The story is visibly autobiographical—Chateaubriand's given name was François-René—and Butor explains that "the dream of becoming a savage is first of all the hope of an erotic liberation" (p. 79).

Upon learning that Louis XVI had been taken prisoner in the Revolution, Chateaubriand returned to France, thereby reinserting himself into the European-Christian value system. He embarked on a long career in politics and literature. When in 1826 he decided to publish a new edition of the *Essai sur les révolutions*, his youthful writing about America was an embarrassment to him: "I am seized by a kind of terror at the sight of my enormous fecundity. In my youth the days must have had more than twenty-four hours for me: no doubt some demon lengthened the time I spent on my diabolical task" (p. 60). Whenever he returned to his youthful works, it was in an attempt to repress their energy and eroticism and to rewrite them so as to confirm the nationalist and Catholic values that he had espoused. *Les Natchez*, of which *René* was originally a part, was not published until 1826; Chateaubriand had to revise the story of the Natchez Indian revolt of 1730 against the French colonists to favor France and the Church—the opposite of the side he takes in the original text.

Chateaubriand, then, like Léon Delmont, illustrates the situation of the modern European, who is a battleground in "the war between two contradictory systems of values, between two traditions, the 'Christian' and the 'pagan'; a war that makes it necessary to keep nature forever at a distance, since whatever aspect of nature either side displays is condemned by the other" (p. 83). It is important to Butor's argument that Chateaubriand realizes that in Native Americans he is not observing "man in a state of nature" but civilizations and cultures that have developed in isolation from Europe. If the Indians were in a state of nature, it might be thought that Europeans could become like them by accessing some hidden harmony in themselves, submerged but permanent because it is natural. In fact, though, the Indians are cultural entities, and modern Europeans can no more become Indians than they can become ancient Greeks or Romans (p. 84).

Modern American culture is of European origin, and it appears in *Niagara* that the promise of America, of a place removed from Europe where people can be free, is lost. Niagara Falls still fascinates by its natural power, and the erotic dimension of that power is reflected in the traditional choice of the falls as a spot for honeymooners. It has also become, however, a place of garish commercialism, and Dean McWilliams explains that "Niagara Falls is one of the ugliest places in North America precisely because it is one of the most beautiful. The seductive power of this natural spectacle is too great; since it cannot be destroyed or hidden, it must be defaced."[16] The lovers in *Niagara* who come to Niagara Falls, whether newlyweds or an older couple returning to the falls to revitalize their lives, do not find what they have come for. Most of the exchanges among them have a distant, isolated quality that stems from the failure of human contact. The final exchange is this one:

What were you saying?	ALFRED
. . .	
Me?	BEATRICE
. . .	
Of course, you.	ALFRED
I said something?	BEATRICE
I thought so.	ALFRED
I don't remember.	BEATRICE (p. 267)

Niagara does not end with the optimistic outlook of *A Change of Heart*; indeed, the text just cited has something of the no-way-out quality of Samuel Beckett's plays. But Butor's vision remains fundamentally positive and committed. If human beings perceive reality through culture, culture can certainly set enormous obstacles between people and their happiness. But culture is not destiny; it can be explained, understood, and finally changed. That is the purpose of a book like *Niagara*, as it is of the book that Léon Delmont hopes to write. Butor is a committed and optimistic writer, as he shows in the conclusion of his essay "Research on the Technique of the Novel": through the architecture of *The Human Comedy*, Balzac allows the reader the mobility of approaching the work from different angles. Butor's hope is to go further: "[B]ut we can conceive of a higher mobility, equally precise and well-defined, the reader becoming responsible for what happens in the microcosm of the work, largely without his realizing it, of course, as in reality, each of his steps, of his choices, taking and giving meaning, enlightening him about his liberty. Someday, without a doubt, we shall reach that point."[17]

6

Claude Simon

It is a measure of the decline of interest in the New Novel that when Claude Simon won the Nobel prize for literature in 1985, his selection was greeted with as little enthusiasm in the French press as in the American. *L'Express* hailed the first French literary Nobel in more than 20 years by calling Simon "the most boring writer since [the nineteenth-century poet and dramatist] Casimir Delavigne," and the *New York Times* noted that in his response to a survey on Claude Simon, Isaac Bashevis Singer asked if the French writer were a man or a woman.[1] On a more serious but equally withering note, *Time* published a quotation from one of Simon's famously long sentences, concluding not that he was another obscure and unfathomable French writer but that it was all rather old hat: "Such sentences may have dazzled the cognoscenti twenty years ago. From the perspective of 1985, both the French new novel and the Nobel given to one of its exemplars seem a bit *anciens*."[2] And Simon, who prefers giving written answers to questions about his work to giving live interviews, may not have helped his case when he provided reporters with a quote that might have worked in a different context but which sounds pretty flat when quoted in English in an American newspaper: "I have discovered that everything means nothing and that ultimately there is nothing to say. I have no message."[3]

Moreover, 1985 was an unfortunate year for a New Novelist to be awarded the Nobel prize, for it seemed that traditional novelists were being celebrated everywhere. The French government had declared 1985 to be "L'Année Hugo" to celebrate the centennial of Victor Hugo's death; the festivities began on January 3 and lasted well into the following year. New biographies, editions of collected works, and special issues of literary journals were published at frequent intervals. And as though it were not enough to have the literary scene dominated by the author of *Les Misérables* and *Notre-Dame de Paris*, the French also celebrated in 1985 the centennial of the *births* of François Mauriac, André Maurois, and Jules Romains, who, while not exactly inheritors of Victor Hugo, would figure prominently in any demonstration that the traditional realist novel thrives in the twentieth century.

Matters were not improved by the scandal associated with Simon's Nobel. In 1983, a member of the Swedish Academy, Artur Lundkvist, broke with tradition by telling reporters that in his opinion, that year's winner, William Golding, did not deserve the prize and that Claude Simon should have been honored, in part because of his supposed influence on Latin American writers. To the general embarrassment caused by Lundkvist's indiscretion was thus added the indirect suggestion—coming from a supporter—that the site of interesting experimental fiction had shifted from France to Latin America, and that Simon's work was to be valued for its influence rather than its own qualities.

In the critical community, on the other hand, some very good work was done about Claude Simon in the 1980s. This is especially significant because Simonian criticism got off to a rather slow start, at least in terms of quantity: the first full-length studies devoted exclusively to his novels did not appear until 1975.[4] There are a number of reasons for this lag, but chief among them is probably that Simon was not much given to theory in the New Novel's formative years, and thus there was no well-defined, provocative framework in which to situate his novels. Jacques Guicharnaud, writing about Simon in the 1959 special issue of *Yale French Studies* devoted to the New Novel, portrays a critical activity that tended to center on theoretical issues:

As one of the group, Claude Simon has not reached the magnitude of Butor or Robbe-Grillet, despite the fact that his last two books, *Le Vent* and *L'Herbe*, were generally praised by the critics. . . . There is no doubt that his technique is not as geometrically defined as Robbe-Grillet's, nor has he invented a gimmick as striking as that of Butor's *La Modification*, nor can any one of his works be summed up in a term as clear-cut as that of "sub-conversation," used to describe Nathalie Sarraute's *Le Planétarium*.[5]

Moreover, Simon was searching for his own technique and style in his early novels; in comparison, the theoretically oriented Robbe-Grillet and the consistent Nathalie Sarraute were more readily linked with a movement whose interest was in large measure theoretical. This lag in work produced about Claude Simon was in a sense beneficial: if prior to the 1980s there was not a huge amount of Simon criticism, neither were there misconceptions like those that continued to plague work about Robbe-Grillet. Furthermore, work about the New Novelists in the 1980s did not have to be done in the hyped, sloganeering atmosphere of the 1960s and 1970s. Many significant studies of Simon's work were produced in the 1980s, both prior to Simon's Nobel prize and afterward.[6]

Simon began writing as early as 1941, but his early works—*Le Tricheur* (*The Cheater;* written in 1941 but published in 1945), *Gulliver* (1952), and *Le Sacre du printemps* (1954)—are experiments that do not attract a great deal of commentary.[7] His next three, *Le Vent* (*The Wind;* 1957), *L'Herbe* (*The Grass;* 1958), and *La Route des Flandres* (*The Flanders Road;* 1960), all published by Les Editions de Minuit, established him as a New Novelist of the phenomenological variety. *The Flanders Road,* which was a considerable success and won the Prix de L'Express, remains the most widely read of Simon's books. After this success, Simon's work moves in the direction taken by the New Novel during its so-called second phase, in which questions of form and textuality gain ascendancy. Works of this period include *Le Palace* (*The Palace;* 1962), *Histoire* (*Histoire;* 1967), and *La Bataille de Pharsale* (*The Battle of Pharsalus;* 1969), the latter firmly establishing this second phase of Simon's work; *Les Corps conducteurs* (*Conducting Bodies;* 1971), *Triptyque* (*Triptych;* 1973), and *Leçon de choses* (*The World About Us;* 1975). His most recent novels, *Les Georgiques* (*The Georgics;* 1981), *L'Invitation* (*The Invitation;* 1987), and *L'Acacia* (*The Acacia;* 1989), are something of a return to his preoccupations of 1960.

The Flanders Road (1960)

The Flanders Road is a curious novel in the sense that it has attracted praise for qualities that one would think were fundamentally antagonistic, if not mutually exclusive. On the one hand, many readers feel that the novel is a powerfully evocative representation of a real occurrence, namely, a small episode in the invading Germans' defeat of the French army in May 1940. Simon participated in this action as a conscripted cavalryman and witnessed the main event that he relates in the novel, the death of a French cavalry captain ambushed by German troops. When the novel was published in 1960, a French officer also present at the captain's death (he appears in the novel as an unnamed second lieutenant) wrote to Simon to congratulate him on the accuracy of his memory and of his descriptions.[8] Other readers, however, admire Simon in general and *The Flanders Road* in particular for the mechanisms by which he calls into question the very ability of human beings to remember and, especially, to narrate any element of the truth. In the final pages of the novel, virtually every assertion by the narrator about the novel's events is accompanied by the question "but how can you tell, how can you tell?" (p. 226).

The narrative perspective is situated in the memory of the character Georges, who remembers scenes from the captain's death, from his own captivity in a prisoner-of-war camp, and from conversations with his comrades Blum and Iglésia. The vantage point from which he remembers these scenes is not at all clear at first; only in the last section of the novel, which opens with long passages of intensely erotic prose, does one realize that all these memories occur sometime after the war, and that Georges is in bed with Corinne, the widow of the cavalry captain killed in 1940.

Indeed, one of the features that distinguishes *The Flanders Road* from some of Simon's earlier novels is a general lack of explicit information regarding the narrative circumstances and structure of the book. When a certain remembered scene recalls another, for example, the transition is usually not made explicit. In a newspaper interview given shortly after the novel's publication, Simon makes his purpose clear:

[I]n these few hours of a postwar night that I consider, everything crowds together in Georges's memory: the disaster of May 1940, the death of the captain of his cavalry troop, his captivity, the train taking him to the POW camp, etc. In memory, everything is situated on the same level: dialogue, vision, and emotion coexist. What I tried to do is create a structure that would match this view of things, which would allow me to present sequentially elements that in reality are superimposed, to come up with a purely sensory architecture. . . . Painters are fortunate indeed: a passerby needs only an instant to become aware of the different elements of a canvas. . . . I was haunted by two things: the discontinuity, the fragmentary character of the emotions one feels, which are never connected to one another, and at the same time their contiguity in consciousness.[9]

In this quotation Simon establishes obvious connections between himself and the other New Novelists. As Lucien Dällenbach points out, Simon's desire to add a *spatial* dimension to narrative is apparent here and is reminiscent of Butor's attempts to take advantage of the nonlinear possibilities of the book.[10] The interest in portraying the discontinuous and fragmentary nature of images that arise in consciousness and in memory is a point in common with Robbe-Grillet as well as with Butor and Sarraute, and the portrayal itself reflects the generally phenomenological nature of Simon's understanding of human consciousness. Indeed, Merleau-Ponty was much taken with Simon's novels and used examples from them to illustrate his lectures.[11] Conversely, many of Simon's ideas about the novel, such as his statement that "What may be written is not the external world, but its projection in us," show the imprint of Merleau-Ponty's work.[12]

An example of Simon's narrative discontinuities will give a good idea of his prose. The following passage is one of the few places in the first section of the novel that show that Georges is in bed with Corinne, remembering scenes from different times in the past:

> . . . realizing then that it wasn't to Blum that he was trying to explain all this [Georges has been relating an event that took place prior to his capture], whispering in the darkness, and not the cattle car either [in which the POWs were transported], the narrow air-hole blocked by the heads or rather the blobs jostling each other noisily, but a single head now that he could touch merely by raising his hand as a blind man recognizes and doesn't even need to bring his hand closer to know in the darkness, smelling the warmth, the breath, breathing the air coming out of the faint dark flower of the lips, the whole face like a kind of dark flower leaning over his as if it were trying to read to divine. . . . But he seized her wrist before she reached him, grasping the other hand in the air, her breasts rolling over his chest: they struggled a moment . . . (pp. 73–74)

In many respects the merging of different layers of the past is reminiscent of Proust, all the more that the merging takes place in bed, as it does in the opening pages of *A la Recherche du Temps perdu* (*Remembrance of Things Past*). Proust is an influence that Simon has always acknowledged readily, as have many of the New Novelists, but in Simon's case the affinity seems to show up in specific intertextual echoes. The absence of explicit transitions from one point in the past to another is a technique unlike Proust's, however, and is widespread in the New Novel. Another affinity recognized by Simon and visible in this passage is with Faulkner, in the long sentences (a Proustian element as well).

A well-known anecdote about the writing of *The Flanders Road* holds that Simon used different-colored pencils to keep the various threads clear in his own mind, and the reader who approaches the novel knowing this may wish that the printer had had the generosity to use colored inks. But the legend of these pencils is more tantalizing than actual fact. Simon explained that after he had written about half of the text (not necessarily the first half of the novel as published), he began to think about putting it all together; to help himself do this, he assigned a color to each character and to each theme and summarized each page on a scrap of paper with the appropriate color. Then he arranged all the scraps of paper on a sheet of plywood to see how the novel might go together, the colors permitting him to see at a glance where each element was.[13] So Simon did not actually compose the text in different colors, and colored inks would not provide a means of "decoding" the novel, of reconstituting a classically readable text, as the first-time reader might innocently think. In any case, as the passage quoted above shows, Simon's dislocations are most often baffling only at first: if the "single head" and "breath" are at first unclear, by the end of the passage the reader knows fairly well what is happening. It is not that with patience the reader can reconstitute a clear, classical story—the very point of the novel is that not even the author can do that—but the reader learns quickly that Simon's point is not to halt his or her progress through the text nor to tease him or her with an unsolvable puzzle. His point is rather to show, on several levels, the relationship between an ordering consciousness and a disordered world.

Simon presents war as the ultimate disordering principle, or rather the ultimate evidence that the world is disordered. When Captain de Reixach is killed by the German machine gunner, he is

sitting as straight and stiff on his saddle as if he had been reviewing his men in the Fourteenth of July parade and not in full retreat or rather rout or rather disaster in the middle of this collapse of everything as if not an army but the world itself the whole world and not only in its physical reality but even in the representation the mind can make of it (but maybe it was the lack of sleep too, the fact that we had had almost no sleep at all in ten days except on horseback) was actually falling apart collapsing breaking up into pieces dissolving into water into nothing . . . (p. 16)

Here the precision and order of a military parade is contrasted with the actual experience of war. Later in the novel, Georges imagines the discrepancy between the understanding of a general officer, who of course has studied warmaking and made it his profession, and what has actually happened to his troops:

[A]nd then when he learned, that is when he realized, finally understood that his brigade no longer existed, had been not annihilated, destroyed according to the rules—or at least what he thought were the rules—of war: normally, correctly, as for instance, by attacking an impregnable position or even by an artillery pounding, or even—he might have accepted this as a last resort—submerged by an enemy attack: but so to speak absorbed, diluted, dissolved, erased from the general-staff charts without his knowing where nor how nor when . . . (p. 151).

At the end of the novel, Georges imagines the general committing suicide by firing a bullet, aptly enough, into his brain (p. 221).

Another suicide, or at least a possible one, occupies much of the novel and much of Georges's thinking. Captain de Reixach's insouciant manner riding into the ambush and his absurd gesture of drawing his saber at the moment of his death suggest to Georges that exposing himself thus to enemy fire was the captain's means of committing suicide. His possible motive for doing so involves another of Georges's preoccupations: the captain's orderly, Iglésia, who was a jockey working for him in civilian life and had a long affair with the captain's young wife, Corinne. One of the scenes that Georges and Blum get Iglésia to tell them about is the prewar horse race in which de Reixach insists on riding the horse usually ridden by Iglésia; the captain loses the race, and the suggestive possibilities of the situation are fully exploited in the text: Iglésia rides horses better than his employer, just as he "mounts" Corinne (they make love hurriedly in the stables) better than her husband does (p. 138). Although de Reixach never confronts Iglésia or Corinne, he comes so close to catching them in flagrante delicto that it is possible, even likely, that he knows. Suicide may be de Reixach's way of dealing with this knowledge.

As in many of Robbe-Grillet's novels, the situation here, in which Georges tries to decide, based on rather slender evidence, whether the captain committed suicide or not, brings to the foreground the problem of the intelligibility of the world. Not only is the conclusion—suicide or not—a difficult determination to make, but even the most dramatic evidence, Iglésia's tale, may be a fabrication. And considering the corrosive effects of war and time on human consciousness, one cannot be certain of anything. The focus of Georges's speculations is a single moment of human history, an enigma "in the center of which he rode ignoring or wanting to ignore what had happened as well as what would happen, in that kind of nothingness (as it is said that in the centre, the eye of the hurricane there exists a perfectly calm zone) of knowledge, that zero point" (p. 231). How can you tell? It may be that the captain rode so slowly not out of a desire to be shot but simply to spare his exhausted horse (p. 229). Indeed, maybe Georges has dreamt the whole affair: "But did I really see him or think I saw him or merely imagine him afterwards or even only dream it all, perhaps I was asleep had I never stopped sleeping eyes wide open in broad daylight lulled by the monotonous hammering of the shoes of the five horses . . ." (p. 231).

Further complications compound the uncertainty of Georges's conjectures. Georges's mother, Sabine, is a de Reixach, but on her mother's side: she has inherited the family mansion but not the name (p. 43). Georges and his captain are thus distantly related, and for both Georges and his mother the de Reixach name, to which they are not entitled but with which they have a certain connection, has a legendary quality, based in antiquity and nobility (one thinks of young Marcel's fascination with the name Guermantes in *A la Recherche du Temps perdu*). Among the possessions inherited with the mansion is a portrait that fascinates Georges during his childhood.[14] It represents an eighteenth-century ancestor who, according to legend, is supposed to have committed suicide. Indeed, the painted figure has a red streak running down its face, so impressing the child Georges with the mystery of violent death that he half expects to see spattered blood on the walls of the room in which the portrait hangs (p. 47). In fact, however, the child is misled by the painting on two scores: first, the ancestor is supposed to have killed himself with a pistol, not a rifle as Georges assumes because the painted figure is posed in hunting costume with a rifle cradled in his arms; second, the red streak on the painting is not the representation of a bullet wound at all but "the reddish-brown preparation of the canvas

revealed by a long crack in the paint's surface" (p. 46). The painting
thus becomes an intersection of many of *The Flanders Road*'s important themes. Like the death of his twentieth-century descendant, the
ancestor's suicide is highly ambiguous, being the product of child-
ish imagination (of bloodstained walls) and perception (of the
painted "wound"). The problem of memory is present too, since the
crack in the painting is a defect due to the canvas's age, as is the
general problem of representation, since the painting represents a
suicide to young Georges through a flaw in the medium.

Another conception that is threatened with collapse under the
stress of war is that of personal identity. In some of the novel's
scenes this theme is stated directly, as when Georges looks at his
image in a mirror without recognizing it (pp. 85, 154), but most of
the novel can be linked with this theme indirectly. A doubling of the
relationship between de Reixach and Georges is suggested: the man
about whom Georges speculates almost to the point of obsession is a
relative who is connected to images from Georges's childhood; after
the war he momentarily takes that relative's place in Corinne's bed.
Another double is mentioned explicitly in the text, in a scene that
takes place in the prisoner-of-war camp in which Georges and Blum
speculate about de Reixach. Georges reflects that he may not in fact
be speaking with Blum "but with himself, that is, his double, all
alone under the grey rain, among the rails, the coal wagons, or perhaps years later, still alone (although he was lying now beside a
woman's warm flesh), still having a dialogue with that double, or
with Blum, or with no one" (p. 139). Just as spatial coordinates are
disrupted, so too are the conventional boundaries of identity. In the
ensuing part of the conversation, it is no longer clear who says
what: "and Blum (or Georges): 'Are you through?,' and Georges (or
Blum): 'I could go on' " (p. 140).

The suspension of identity takes place on the level of narrative
structure, too: *The Flanders Road* begins with Georges as first-person narrator, who uses the pronoun "I." After the first few pages,
which are devoted to the scene of the captain's death and some
related scenes involving the captain, the narrator abruptly and
without explanation begins referring to himself (presumably) as
"Georges" (p. 24); in the rest of the novel, Simon switches back and
forth between the two modes. Obviously this shift has something
to do with the question of identity, and an immediate clue is
given by the scene in which the shift first occurs. Georges's unit,

exhausted, is on the march when he sees on the road the remains of a dead horse:

and that must have been where I saw it for the first time, a little before or a little after we stopped to drink, discovering it, staring at it through that kind of half-sleep, that kind of brownish mud in which I was somehow caught, and maybe because we had to detour to avoid it, and actually sensing it more than seeing it: I mean (like everything lying along the road: the trucks, the cars, the suitcases, the corpses) something unexpected, unreal, hybrid, so that what had been a horse (that is, what you knew, what you could recognize as having been a horse) was no longer anything now but a vague heap of limbs, of dead meat, of skin and sticky hair, three-quarters covered with mud—*Georges* wondering without exactly finding an answer ... (pp. 23–24; my italics)

The horse has not only died but ceased to belong to the category "horse," ceased to be identifiable as anything, so that even the words "dead horse" seem not to apply. Later in the passage Simon describes the dead animal as not so much decomposing as simply being reabsorbed by the earth, disappearing into the primordial, undifferentiated matter from which it came. The horse is covered with mud, even though it has not rained recently, as though Mother Earth were reaching out "before slowly and definitely engulfing it in its breast" (p. 24). Since the narrator compares his fatigued state to "that kind of brownish mud in which I was somehow caught," the image is of Georges, too, submerging his identity into the womblike earth.

Thus the shift in narration from first to third person signifies a dispersion of identity under the disrupting effects of war. This technique attracted the attention of Merleau-Ponty, who saw it as Simon's creation of an "intermediate person" between first and third.[15] Such a nontraditional concept of the ego corresponds to Merleau-Ponty's phenomenology: if consciousness is consciousness of something, it becomes difficult to speak of an ego already fully constituted perceiving the world when that ego can discover itself only during the process of perception:

I cannot say that *I* perceive the blue sky in the same way that I say that I understand a book or that I decide to devote my life to mathematics. My perception, even seen from within, expresses a given situation: I see the blue of the sky because I am *sensitive* to colors. . . . Every sensation has an element of dream or of depersonalization as we feel it by that sort of stupor into which it puts us when we truly live at its level.[16]

Simon's rectification in the dead-horse passage, "actually *sensing* it more than *seeing* it," seems to echo Merleau-Ponty ("I am *sensitive* to colors"), just as the overall mood of the passage seems to communicate precisely the "stupor" that Merleau-Ponty describes. Merleau-Ponty is however describing human perception in general; the only specificity he mentions in the passage cited above is "when we truly live at its level." Although war in *The Flanders Road* has a special effect on its participants, it is an effect that only makes more apparent the fundamental situation of human consciousness: war obliges Simon's characters to "live on the level" of humanity's relation to the world.

The encounter with the dead horse is intended by Simon to be key to the novel. In an interview given in 1960, he explained how he hit on the book's form (trained as a painter, Simon is much given to visual metaphors when describing his fiction):

[At first] I couldn't *see* this book at all. I perceived only simultaneous emotions arising in my mind; everything presented itself at the same time. Only later did its composition appear to me as I thought about the form of the ace of clubs which cannot be drawn without lifting pencil from paper except by passing three times through the same point. That point, in *The Flanders Road*, is the dead horse toward which the cavalrymen return three times in their wandering.[17]

Thus the scene of the dead horse occurs four times in the novel (as Vivian Mercier points out, if the soldiers *return* to it three times, there are four iterations in all), constituting a sort of center. Horses are a thematic and symbolic center as well, what with the prewar horse races, the jockeys' racing colors being linked with clothes strewn on the road by fleeing civilians, the sound of the horses' hooves representing the passage of time, Iglésia "mounting" his employer's horse and wife, and so on. But as Joyce Loubère observes, whereas all this horse signifying may be the novel's structural center, it does not lead to a fixed meaning:

None of these combinations [horses and time, sex] take precedence over the others; they form groups that tend to combine with other groups. They offer no explanations and no parables. These combinations in all their density impose a pattern on the narration, but that pattern signifies the failure of the mind to impose on them all collectively a satisfying order, or a definitive meaning.[18]

Making approximately the same point, Stephen Heath observes that in the second iteration of the dead-horse scene, the animal is described as having no insides; its wound exposes no internal organs, and it looks like a broken child's toy, "a simple shape surrounding emptiness" (p. 82).[19] The structure of horse symbolism, or better, the novel itself, is hollow in that it contains no kernel of meaning.

As this failure of the signifying process may suggest, on one level *The Flanders Road* is about writing. As Joyce Loubère argues, the novel may be taken to illustrate the various stages in the construction of fiction:[20] the writer's lived experience (the war), other aspects of his life (for example, childhood fascination with the portrait), the attempt to remember, organize, and interpret experience (did the captain commit suicide?). In this regard, the English phrase "how can you tell" has an apt double meaning not present in the French "comment savoir": both "how can one know," which is how the French phrase would be translated literally, and "how can one tell," that is, *recount* or *narrate*.

Attention is drawn to this level of interpretation not only by the fact that *The Flanders Road* is a novel based partly on Claude Simon's experience but chiefly by two central reflexive devices: Georges's relations with his father and the nature of his conversations with Blum.

Georges's father is a humanist (a professor, perhaps) whom Georges remembers spending August afternoons in a summerhouse, writing amidst mounds of old papers. Georges is bitterly sarcastic about his father's belief in Western civilization: "he's deeply convinced that there's no problem, and particularly no problem standing in the way of humanity's happiness, that can't be solved by reading good authors" (p. 165). It is clear that in Georges's estimation at least, the father's belief in books is a quasireligious ordering principle, a means, conscious or not, of saving himself from the chaotic and meaningless truth of human existence:

But he's suffering and trying to hide it to keep up his courage too That's why he's talking so much Because all he can manage is that ponderous stubborn and superstitious credulity—or rather faith—in the absolute preeminence of knowledge acquired by proxy, of what is written down, of those words which his own father who was only a peasant had never managed to decipher, lending them, charging them with a kind of mysterious magical power . . . (p. 31)

Although it is at least suggested that Georges's disdain for his father's values goes back some time, it is the war that provides the most flagrant evidence of the father's error in believing in "useless and empty words" (p. 31). In the German prison camp Georges receives a letter from his father deploring the bombing of Leipzig and its great library. Whereas the father's values transcend political conflict, Georges replies to him that the war refutes those values: if the Leipzig library, with its thousands upon thousands of volumes, contained nothing that might prevent its own destruction, it was not of much use (p. 166). He concludes his letter with a list of the "positive values" that humanity really needs: "shoes, underwear, wool clothes, soap, cigarettes, sausage . . ." (p. 166).

Indeed, the war questions not only the capacity of books to articulate transcendent values but even the power of words to describe: in a passage quoted earlier, "annihilated" and "destroyed" do not adequately convey what happened to the general's brigade, nor does any single word. Rather, Simon uses one of his verbal proliferations or rectifications: "absorbed, diluted, dissolved, erased" (p. 151). Such series of words or expressions are highly characteristic of the text of *The Flanders Road*. Sometimes the hesitation among different terms is explicit, expressed by such phrases as "or rather" or "I mean," as when Georges sees the image of his face in the mirror: "my or rather that ghastly face" (p. 36). Very often, however, the descriptive terms are simply multiplied, without punctuation, as when Captain de Reixach learns that he is related to Georges: "he said I think we're cousins more or less, but in his mind I suppose that as far as I was concerned the word probably meant something more like mosquito insect midge" (p. 11). In general, the device signifies the difficulty of description or expression; the last example, in which the alternative terms do not appreciably improve on the first, comes close to suggesting the impossibility of expressing truth in language. As in the case of the horse imagery, Simon uses multiple words without suggesting that such rectification or sorting will ever result in a single, unified meaning.

Georges is not as ambitious as his father; whereas the latter looks confidently to language for eternal truth, Georges would be content to learn merely what happened. Obstacles in this pursuit are the destructive effect of time on memory and of war on comprehension. Another obstacle, one more connected with language itself, is revealed principally in Georges's conversations in the prison camp with Blum: fabulation. Blum and Georges have to prod and coax Iglésia so much to hear the story of his affair with Corinne that they cannot be at all sure that the story is true. When Iglésia does yield to their entreaties, he tends to express himself in grunts and monosyllables, and Blum embroiders the story of the horse race in a lurid passage that parodies bad erotic fiction in order to suggest that Georges is not really interested in the truth (p. 138). When Georges objects, Blum responds: "Fine, sorry. I thought you enjoyed it: you're always sifting, supposing, embroidering, inventing fairy tales where I bet no one except you has ever seen anything but an everyday piece of sex" (p. 138). That Blum should embroider Iglésia's story is not surprising, since he "knows" as much as Georges; but when he begins frenziedly to spin tales around the portrait of Georges's dead ancestor (pp. 141–50), one is obliged to think that something remarkable is going on. Blum is of course referred to as Georges's double, and what is being suggested is that Blum's mythomania and Georges's desire to know the truth are really one and the same: " 'Wasn't it like that?,' and Georges: 'No!,' and Blum: 'No? But what do you know about it?,' and Georges: 'No!,', and Blum [continues]" (p. 148).

Thus there may be nothing more to Georges's attempted comprehension of the past than the need to tell stories, the attraction of words: "boasts gossip obscenities words sounds just to keep us awake to deceive ourselves into thinking we were awake to encourage each other, Blum saying now: But maybe that gun wasn't even loaded maybe he didn't even know how to use it People like making everything into a tragedy a drama a novel . . ." (p. 205). Another possibility, one that occupies a much greater role in Simon's later fiction, is that the glimpses of signification that Georges has been pursuing originate not only from a desire to transform life into tragedy but from within language itself. Perhaps the vision of Corinne that obsesses him throughout his captivity, and it is Corinne who is at the center of all of Georges's interpretations, comes into being from a verbal association:

standing with the sun behind her at the end of the afternoon in that red dress the colour of a gumdrop (but perhaps he had invented that too, that is the colour, the harsh red, perhaps merely because she was something he thought about not with his mind but with his lips, his mouth, perhaps because of her name, because "Corinne" made him think of "coral"?) (p. 174)

At any rate, the novel ends with images of the failure of Georges's quest. The last time he sees the dead horse, it is a thing truly devoid of meaning, a bit of scenery in a play that has finished its last performance: "after all it was only a dead horse, a piece of carrion just good enough for the knacker: probably he would come by here along with the ragpickers and the scrap-iron men the dustmen picking up the forgotten or outmoded props now that the actors and the audience had gone, the sounds of the cannon fading too . . ." (p. 227). The novel's last sentence is a clear echo of the final sentence of *Remembrance of Things Past*, ending as it does with the word "time," but whereas Proust's last sentence is one of hope and triumph, of vision restored and time conquered, Simon's is characterized by images of decay and fragmentation: "the whole landscape empty uninhabited under the motionless sky, the whole world stopped frozen crumbling collapsing gradually disintegrating in fragments like an abandoned building, unusable, left to the incoherent, casual, impersonal and destructive work of time" (p. 231).

Simon's working title for the novel published as *The Flanders Road* was *Fragmentary Description of a Disaster*, with which one can readily contrast the organic wholeness of time recaptured and artistic vision confirmed in Proust. A *fragmentary* description, the novel questions assumptions about representational fiction; but the *disaster* of May 1940 itself stands for a fragmented reality, and the evocative power of the book lies in the very incoherence and discontinuity of Georges's memory. In 1960, Simon had not yet begun to question the assumptions of the novel in a sustained and direct manner; in his next few novels, questions of *écriture* and textuality come to the fore.

Triptych (1973)

In the 1960s and early 1970s much of the critical activity having to do with the New Novel was structuralist in nature, as exemplified by Jean Ricardou's distinction between a realist fiction whose aim is "the writing of an adventure" and a reflexive fiction in which one finds "the adventure of writing."[21] Thus is inaugurated what some have called the second phase of the New Novel, in which the antireferential tendency of the genre comes to the fore: writing does not represent anything so much as its own mechanisms.

Like Robbe-Grillet, Claude Simon was much influenced by this body of thought, and it is at this point that he begins to write his few theoretical texts. Chief among these is the preface to *Orion aveugle* (*Blind Orion*), published in 1970, in which he explains his conception of the creative process of writing:

> For my part, I know no other paths of creation than those opened up step by step, that is, word after word, by the progress itself of writing.
>
> Before I begin to trace signs on paper there is nothing, save a formless magma of more or less confused sensations, an accumulation of more or less precise memories, and a vague—very vague—project.[22]

This phase of the New Novel produced some very quotable statements, and Simon proved himself the equal of any writer. Once, when asked what problems he was preoccupied with, he replied that he had three problems: how to begin a sentence, how to continue it, and how to end it.[23]

The pithier the statement of nonreferential textual autonomy, of course, the harder it is to reconcile with Simon's early novels, such as *The Flanders Road*, which seems in the final analysis still to *represent* something. Simon doubtless had—as did Robbe-Grillet—something of a tendency to revise past texts in the light of current theory. Further, some of his statements can seem contradictory: "Formerly, I used to say that it is possible to reconstruct from lived, felt experience. Today, after having thought about this, I no longer think that one can *reconstruct* anything whatsoever. What one *constructs* is a text, and this text corresponds to only one thing: what is happening in the writer at the moment that he writes."[24] Up to the last clause, this statement is a fairly typical structuralist-phase rejection of representation. But the last idea, that the text does indeed "correspond to something" in the writer, could be taken to be an attenuated statement of many theories of composition that the New Novel purports to reject, specifically the psychological realism or phenomenological realism that is supposedly confined to first-phase New Novels. After all, if what is in Claude Simon as he writes *The Flanders Road* is memories, however uncertain, of actual lived experience, the book is arguably representational, referential, and a reconstruction, although to insist on these aspects to the exclusion of all others is as great an error as it is to deny them.

Leaving aside the question of revisionism, the novels that Simon produced in the 1970s work very effectively with antireferential ideas, and are indeed a good deal more compelling than some of the glib theoretical claims that came from Simon and others. *Triptych* is a excellent case in point.

An alert reader can perhaps see where Simon is headed from the very beginning of the novel, which describes a scene depicted on a postcard that is itself an object in a description, a sort of still life:

The postcard shows an esplanade bordered by a row of palm trees standing out against a sky of too bright a blue, at the edge of a sea of too bright a blue. A long cliff of blinding white façades, with rococo decorations, follows the curve of the bay in a gently-sweeping arc. Exotic shrubbery and clusters of cannas are planted between the palm trees, forming a bouquet in the foreground of the photograph. . . . The inking of the various colors does not precisely coincide with the contours of each of the objects, so that as a consequence the harsh green of the palm trees overlaps the blue of the sky, or the mauve of a scarf or a parasol encroaches on the ocher of the ground or the cobalt of the sea. The postcard is lying on the corner of a kitchen table covered with yellow, red, and pink checkered oilcloth, nicked in several places by the blades of cleavers or knives that have slipped. . . . Not far from the postcard, the pink body of a skinned rabbit is stretched out on a porcelain platter with thick edges.[25]

The reflexive aspects of this passage are multiple. The postcard is a photograph, the most realistic of the visual arts, but the colors are "too bright" and technical difficulties of color printing have intruded into the scene, since the colors are out of register. Photographs are naively thought to portray things exactly as they are, but the word "rococo" reminds the reader that there are different styles in art, and indeed that the main purpose of art is often not to represent but to decorate. "Cobalt" blue and "ocher" are artists' colors, again perhaps contaminating the notion of purely realistic photography with an allusion to painting. That the postcard portrays a scene and is in turn portrayed *in* a scene draws attention to the process of representation, undermining it and stressing that none of what we are reading is visual description of any kind but verbal. The two levels (postcard scene and kitchen scene) even interpenetrate one another, the postcard's foreground flowers like a bouquet of flowers *set on the table* to complete the still life composition: "Skinned Rabbit, with Flowers."

From the interior of the kitchen, the descriptive point of view moves outdoors, and there follows a description of the village in which the house is located, a river, a waterfall and sawmill, a church, and finally a barn that has circus posters pasted on its exterior walls. Two boys, watching a trout in the clear river from a vantage point on a bridge, are introduced. Then there occurs the first of the many abrupt scene changes that constitute the book's principle means of moving forward:

One of the boys stretches out his arm, one finger pointing in the direction of the trout, and the reflection of his torso moves closer to that of the other boy. Although neither one of them has spoken, the trout darts to the right with a rapid flick of its tail and slips through the mouth of the pitcher lying on its side. Before it disappears, the boys manage to catch a glimpse of its gleaming light-colored underbelly. When the man's pelvis moves backward, one glimpses for the fraction of a second his gleaming cylindrical member partly emerging from the thick black tuft of hair between his bent thighs, which look faintly blue, like skim milk, and phosphorescent in the yellowish half-light of the barn. One of the boys warns the other in a whisper not to move and it will soon come out again. (p. 7)

Prior to this scene, the reader has learned that there are cracks in the wood of the barn wall, some appearing to have been enlarged by a knife blade, so it is not too difficult to understand that the scene has shifted from the river to a couple making love in the barn, witnessed by the two boys peering through the widened crack. At the end of the passage quoted above, the scene shifts back to the river, the last sentence a humorously ambiguous transition.

It is interesting to note the mechanisms or motivation of the scene shift: the transition seems occasioned by analogies between the trout and the man's penis, analogies of movement, shape, and lighting. In view of Georges's suggestion in *The Flanders Road* that perhaps his vision of Corinne stems from his association of her name with coral, it is important to note here that the words "glimpse" and "gleaming" are applied to both scenes. This doubling of words occurs often in these abrupt transitions and is doubtless an example of what Simon meant by the creative possibilities opened up by writing:

Each word provokes (or calls for) many others, not only by the force of the images that it draws to itself like a magnet, but also sometimes by its morphology alone, simple assonances, as well as the formal requirements of syntax, rhythm and composition, often turn out to be as fruitful as its multiple meanings.[26]

From fragments such as the ones already discussed, the reader little by little can identify three or four stories from *Triptych*. A servant girl and a farm laborer make love in a barn, observed by two boys; a drunken young man on the eve of his wedding makes love to a barmaid in an alley behind the bar; a nude woman lies on a bed in a hotel room, apparently pleading with a man to intercede on behalf of her son, who is in trouble with the police over a drug charge. The fourth set of images, the performance of a clown in a circus, is less a story than the others. The first narrative is the one with the most elements: the servant girl, seeing her lover approaching, asks the two boys to tend the little girl with her (her daughter?); the boys, eager to spy on the lovers, in turn give the little girl to some other children, who neglect her. From subsequent scenes of the young woman's grief and of a search of the river and its banks, we gather that the little girl has drowned.

Thus in some respects *Triptych* resembles *The Flanders Road*: there are more or less brusque transitions among a series of narratives, and a degree of uncertainty about the events that actually transpire. But in the earlier novel, one can determine a certain hierarchy of events in the sense that Georges really *is* in bed with Corinne, after the war. Other scenes that the reader may think he or she is witnessing directly turn out to be either Georges's memories, such as Captain de Reixach's death or his memories of other characters' possibly fallacious testimony, such as Iglésia's hurried coupling with Corinne in the stables. *The Flanders Road* still turns on a fundamental ambiguity, since Georges cannot determine the truth behind the captain's death, but the relationship between narrative and reality is comparatively straightforward. In *Triptych*, Simon goes to a new level of ambiguity in his attitude toward literary representation.

In one of the iterations of the scene of the nude woman in the hotel room, there appears on the wall next to the head of her male companion an engraving depicting the interior of a barn, with a servant girl and a farmhand about to make love on a pile of hay. The scene is observed by two laughing boys, whose faces one can see framed in the barn's window (pp. 28–29). The scene is not quite identical to the one narrated in *Triptych*, since the boys are looking through a window, not a crack in the wall, but it is close enough to constitute a playful *mise en abyme* that suggests that the boundaries of fact and fiction, reality and representation, are blurred.

But this playfulness is only a preparation for *Triptych*'s central reflexive device: each narrative sequence is revealed to be fictive, a representation of one kind or another, indeed of one kind *after* another. Thus the hotel room in which the nude woman lies on a bed is transformed into a movie set, and thence into a *painting* of a movie set:

The eyes are open in the upturned face, staring fixedly at the ceiling of the room, or rather, the flies above the studio stage with their cables, their winches, their catwalks equipped with floodlights. In accordance with a classical technique, the artist, with the aid of a Venetian red pigment that lightens to a pink tint on the surfaces in relief, has first sketched the body in monochrome, carefully indicating the anatomical details, as in those plates illustrating ancient treatises on painting, showing the modeling of each of the muscles in the form of spindles or sinews that intertwine, cross and overlap each other. (p. 59)

The sequences contain descriptive details from other sequences, as the idea of anatomical plates here is a reference to descriptions of the skinned rabbit. The fictional representation of one sequence plays a role in the others, as when the two boys examine movie stills containing scenes from the hotel room (p. 58) and the nude woman/actress reads a novel that seems to contain scenes that occur elsewhere in *Triptych* (p. 95). It is not possible to identify one of the sequences as "real," relative to the others. Thus it turns out that the barn is also used as the village movie theater, and in one iteration of the lovemaking scene the film jams in the projector, revealing the scene witnessed by the two boys to be a movie (p. 148). But one cannot conclude that the boys are real and the servant girl fictive, for in other places in the novel, they interact with her and indeed contribute to her daughter's death.

Rather, each sequence in the novel points to the other sequences as fictive, in circular fashion, thus completely invalidating decisions about reality and representation. The novel's final image warns against attempting any definitive reconstruction. The man from the hotel-room sequence appears with a large jigsaw puzzle, almost completed (p. 168). The puzzle represents the village described in the opening pages of *Triptych*, with the two boys and their fishing poles. The man inserts the last piece into the puzzle, looks at it a short while, then dashes the puzzle to the floor, scattering the pieces (p. 171).

If *The Flanders Road* asks, "How can you tell?" mostly in terms of a man trying to make sense of his own experience, *Triptych* extends that questioning to the very grounds of art itself, asking about the nature of representation and the relationship between the object of representation and its mechanisms. Neither novel contains an answer to the question it poses, the necessity of asking the question being the only conclusion that Simon has reached.

7

Marguerite Duras

If the four writers considered thus far in this study figure prominently on virtually everyone's list of New Novelists, the relationship of Marguerite Duras to the New Novel is far more problematical. She was often included in the earliest discussions of the New Novel—her works were treated in both the *Esprit* issue of 1958 and the *Yale French Studies* issue of 1959—but even then, commentators felt it necessary to distinguish between her work and, for example, that of Robbe-Grillet and Sarraute.[1]

One reason for excluding Duras from the New Novel, or at least qualifying her inclusion, is her general refusal to make theoretical claims for her work. Speaking in the context of French feminism of the 1970s, when there was much interest in specifically feminine writing, or *écriture féminine,* Duras declared that obsession with theory was a male trait: "Women have been in the darkness for centuries. They don't know themselves. Or only poorly. And when women write, they translate this darkness. . . . Men don't translate. They begin from a theoretical platform that is already in place, already elaborated."[2] Male patterns of theoretical thought, she asserted, are retrograde: "The criterion on which men judge intelligence is still the capacity to theorize and in all the movements that one sees now [1973], in whatever area it may be, cinema, theater, literature, the theoretical sphere is losing influence. . . . Men must learn to be silent. This is probably very painful for them. To quell their theoretical voice, the exercise of theoretical interpretation."[3] This is not to say that Duras's work is of no theoretical interest, quite the contrary. But the theoretical issues that are often discussed in connection with her work, such as feminism, are generally not raised by the author herself, although she has often participated in such discussions, and are most often not closely related to the largely formal issues of novelistic composition raised by the other New Novelists. Duras herself never wrote a theory of the novel, and one never has the sense, as one can have in the case of certain other New Novelists, that a particular novel was written at least partly in order to make a theoretical point.

Moreover, Duras never claimed membership in the New Novel group and often held herself aloof from it. Perhaps no better example of this aloofness can be found than the following excerpt from an interview with Xavière Gauthier in 1973, in which Duras confuses—or pretends to confuse—Robbe-Grillet and Ricardou:

> Duras: To come back to what the theoretician of the *Nouveau Roman* says—what's his name?
> Gauthier: Robbe-Grillet?
> Duras: No, the one who did *Pour un nouveau roman*, Ricardou.[4]

It is hard to imagine anyone with the slightest interest in the New Novel making such an error.

On the other hand, if a writer's mere desire to be considered a New Novelist should not suffice to make it so, neither can Duras's aloofness obscure the obvious relationship her work has with the rest of the literary and critical community of her time. As Marilyn R. Schuster points out, Duras's works "anticipate, reflect, and shape the major literary problems of the past fifty years. She explored realism (though in an ironic mode) in her early novels, experimented with the dissolution of fictional conventions with the new novel in the late fifties and sixties, made films in the seventies, and engaged in the seduction of autobiography in the eighties."[5]

Described in this way, Duras's trajectory is very much like that of other New Novelists; each of Schuster's four phases is characteristic of at least some of the other writers under consideration here.

Duras's first novels, of which the most famous is *Un Barrage contre le Pacifique* (*The Sea Wall*), published by Gallimard in 1950, are usually thought of as traditional in some sense of that term. *Un Barrage contre le Pacifique* is set in French Indochina, where Duras was born and grew up with her mother and brother (as Marguerite Donnadieu; she took the name Duras in the 1930s). Observers often see a relationship between Duras's early work and the mid-century American novel, particularly works by Hemingway.[6]

The break in Duras's fictional technique is most often reckoned to come with *Le Square* (*The Square;* 1955) in 1955 and *Moderato cantabile* (1958). It is with these novels that Duras's relationship to the New Novel is perhaps closest. Their publication dates correspond perfectly with the first New Novels by other authors and with the beginning of the elaboration of the concept. Significantly, Duras switched from the Gallimard publishing house to the New Novel publisher Jérôme Lindon's Editions de Minuit for *Moderato cantabile*. This novel enjoyed considerable success and is widely read in French schools today, like that other New Novel bestseller, Butor's *A Change of Heart*. The following years brought further innovative novels from Duras: *Dix heures et demie du soir en été* (*10:30 on a Summer Night;* 1960), *L'Après-midi de M. Andesmas* (*The Afternoon of Mr. Andesmas;* 1962) *Le Ravissement de Lol V. Stein* (*The Ravishing of Lol Stein;* 1964), and *Le Vice-Consul* (*The Vice-Consul;* 1965).

At about the time of *Moderato cantabile*, Duras embarked on her first cinema project, the scenario for Alain Resnais's *Hiroshima mon amour*, released in 1959. Resnais was also to be Robbe-Grillet's collaborator for *Last Year at Marienbad* (1960). Much of Duras's creative effort in the 1970s was devoted to film and produced such critical successes as *Détruire, dit-elle* (*Destroy, She Said;* 1969), *Nathalie Granger* (1972), *India Song* (1974), and *Le Camion* (*The Truck;* 1977).

In 1984, Duras produced a huge bestseller, *L'Amant* (*The Lover*), a novel that drew on her youth in colonial Indochina, a subject she had not treated directly since *The Sea Wall*. The book won the Prix Goncourt and sold 700,000 copies before the end of the year. The English translation (*The Lover;* 1985) was equally popular, and Jean-Jacques Annaud transformed the story into a successful movie in 1992. Duras worked for a while on the film but withdrew after a series of disagreements with Annaud. Some of the material she had prepared for the film was incorporated into *L'Amant de la Chine du nord* (*The North China Lover;* 1991).[7]

Thus, at about the time that the press was expressing a degree of incredulity at Claude Simon's Nobel prize, the work of Marguerite Duras was enjoying a huge success. Not only the reading and moviegoing public but also university scholars participated in this boom: far more critical work has been published about Duras in the 1980s and 1990s than about any other New Novelist.

There are no doubt reasons for this success that go beyond the qualities of the work itself. Duras's work intersects with a number of social and academic issues that have gained in importance in the last three decades. Feminism is one of those issues, and although the relationship between Duras and feminist thought has always been somewhat unsettled and controversial, her work is rich ground for readings informed by feminist theory. As was suggested above, Duras herself has participated actively and controversially in discussions of feminism. Her background in Indochina is all the more intriguing due to recent academic and general interest in colonial and postcolonial issues. One might have expected Duras, a white European living in colonial Indochina, to represent herself as having or at least as being associated with imperialist values, but as the daughter of a *poor*, single French woman, Duras saw herself as marginalized by the very colonial system she also represented and saw no problem in characterizing herself as Creole. Finally, Duras's connection with the highly influential psychoanalytic theories of Jacques Lacan has also contributed to the interest in her work in academic circles. Together, feminism, postcolonialism, and Lacanian psychoanalysis inform a huge amount of the scholarly work of the last 25 years, and that all three should come together in a work as successful with the reading public as *The Lover* goes a long way toward explaining why Marguerite Duras's work is today considered much more contemporary than that of any of the other writers associated with the New Novel.

Moderato cantabile (1958)

Moderato cantabile has the most in common with other New Novels of the first phase. As New Novels go, *Moderato cantabile* is not especially difficult to read in the sense of processing the text. For example, the first chapter of the eight that make up this short book recounts in straightforward if remarkably spare fashion a mundane event: a mother takes her reluctant son to his piano lesson.

> "Will you please read what's written above the score?" the lady asked.
> "Moderato cantabile," said the child.
> The lady punctuated his reply by striking the keyboard with a pencil. The child remained motionless, his head turned towards his score.
> "And what does moderato cantabile mean?"
> "I don't know."
> A woman, seated ten feet away, gave a sigh. . . .
> "Madame Desbaresdes, you have a very stubborn little boy."
> Anne Desbaresdes sighed again.
> "You don't have to tell me," she said.[8]

Not only are the events of the story easy to follow, but so is the thematic opposition begun here between the piano teacher as a representative of social roles and obligations (she is referred to as a "lady" and addresses the mother by a social title, "Madame Desbaresdes") and the mother's relationship with her child (the narrator refers to the mother as a "woman" and gives her name as Anne Desbaresdes). That the mother takes her child's side in his rebelliousness is perhaps unexpected but is expressed clearly enough: " 'What a child,' Anne Desbaresdes said happily, 'really, what a child! How in the world did I happen to have such an obstinate ...' " (p. 65). Rather conventional symbols are even brought into play, as when the harassed piano student listens to the sound of a motorboat passing by, a symbol of evasion (p. 64).

It is in the larger sense of the word "reading" that the difficulty of the novel presents itself. On the level of sentence and paragraph, the extreme simplicity of Duras's language produces a kind of transparency, but the spareness of her writing is far more remarkable for what it does *not* say about the final meaning the reader ought to find in the novel as a whole. This elusiveness is the hallmark of Duras's fiction, and it is felt not only by the reader but by the author herself, according to Duras: "Ignorance is the starting point of my work. If I am omniscient I do not write. It is in ignorance, in the impossibility of grasping that I write. I think this is a basic given common to all my books."[9]

At the end of the first chapter, the story begins to get more complicated when the piano lesson is interrupted by a woman's scream in the street below. A man has murdered his wife in a neighborhood café. As an element of the plot the event is simple enough, but it appears to be caught up in unexpected emotional forces, both in the husband, who kisses his dead wife and calls her "darling," and in Anne Desbaresdes, who when she first hears the scream from the piano teacher's apartment attempts to deny its importance ("It's nothing") but in the remaining chapters of the novel returns compulsively several times to the café to learn more about the crime.

In these visits to the café, she talks and drinks wine with a man named Chauvin, and a few more details about her situation emerge. She is the wife of the wealthy director of a nearby industry and thus has a social position well above this working-class café and well above that of Chauvin, who is now unemployed but once worked for her husband. He recognizes her from receptions given for the workers in her home, as indeed do the other patrons of the café and the owner. Anne and Chauvin's meetings in the café scandalize the owner and the other customers.

Why Anne is fascinated by the crime is perhaps the first enigma that the reader encounters. From scattered clues in the text—nothing is ever said directly, by Anne or by Chauvin—the reader gets the idea that she is deeply alienated from her social and domestic situation; the murder seems to represent for her an intensity of feeling that is generally missing from her life. It has already been established that her relationship with her child is something unique in her life and in opposition to her social situation; significantly, then, Anne associates the murdered woman's scream with childbirth: "I think I must have screamed something like that once, yes, when I had the child" (p. 79). But the pain of childbirth is not necessarily a negative memory for Anne, as is suggested when Chauvin follows up on the comparison between the dead woman's scream and Anne's:

"Was it very painful when you had your child?"
"I screamed . . . you have no idea."
She smiled as she remembered, leaned back in her chair, suddenly completely free of her fear. (p. 79)

Nor is the woman's murder negative for Anne. First, there is the husband's behavior with his dead wife, which suggests that whatever his motives for killing her may have been they are connected somehow with passionate love. But more important, Anne and Chauvin's discussion of the crime reveals her somewhat paradoxical attitude toward it. When she first goes to the café the day after the murder, it is under the pretext of an ordinary sort of curiosity, and her first exchanges with Chauvin are in this vein:

"The scream was so loud it's really only natural for people to try and find out what happened. I would have found it difficult not to, you know."
She drank her wine, the third glass.
[Chauvin replies,] "All I know is that he shot her through the heart." (p. 72)

As the conversation continues, however, it is apparent not only that Anne's interest is far greater than idle curiosity and that the point of her visits to the café is not really to find out the truth about the woman who was murdered. As she presses Chauvin for explanations that he cannot give and hazards interpretations that can have no basis in fact, it becomes apparent that Anne and Chauvin's reconstruction of the crime is almost purely fictional. Chauvin freely admits that he knows little about the couple and that he hasn't been able to learn anything further, so when he suggests an explanation for the crime the reader understands that he is in fact attempting to give Anne what she wants:

"I said nothing," the man repeated. "But I think that he aimed at her heart, just as she asked him to."
Anne Desbaresdes sighed. A soft, almost erotic sigh. (p. 75)

In Anne's third visit to the café, they refer explicitly to the imaginary nature of their speculations about the dead woman and her husband: Chauvin says, "Hurry and say something. Make it up" (p. 89).

Scenes like this one, in which a man and a woman talk to each other in elusive terms about their desires and needs, are quite common in Duras's work. In *The Square*, for example, a traveling salesman and a young woman, strangers to each other, discuss their lives in a public square. The salesman relates the insignificance of his existence, the young woman, her hope that some day a man will marry her and thus change her life. At the end of the story when the narrator alludes to the possibility that the man will turn up at the weekly dance that the young woman habitually attends and that both of their lives will thus change, there is the suggestion that the couple moves from a relationship that takes place only in language to reality.

In *Moderato cantabile*, reality and language never manage to sort themselves out (nor do they, really, in *The Square*). At the end of the novel, it becomes clear that Anne and Chauvin want to reenact the crime, if only in language, and that their conversation has been in preparation for this culmination: " 'I wish you were dead,' Chauvin said. 'I am,' Anne Desbaresdes said" (p. 118). (In the French version, Anne says "*C'est fait*"—"it is done," which shows more explicitly than the English translation that the act of murder has been transposed into language). Thereupon Anne turns and walks out of the bar, and the novel ends.

How to read this reenactment of murder is the central enigma of *Moderato cantabile*. One possibility is to consider Duras's testimony about an episode in her own life, a love affair that inspired the novel: "It was an erotic experience that was very, very violent—how do you describe it?—I went through a crisis that was . . . suicidal; that is . . . what I tell in *Moderato cantabile*, this woman who wants to be killed, I lived that."[10] Indeed, there are other autobiographical elements in the novel. Anne's compulsive drinking of red wine in the bar reminds one of Duras's alcoholism, and there are traces of the author's experience with Communism in that this upper-class woman spends time with an unemployed workingman.

But the link between Duras's experience and her books is easy to exaggerate; for that matter, Duras herself often did. Moreover, her allusions to her love affair do not really help much. Anne perhaps wants to commit a kind of suicide, as Duras may have, but the link between desire and suicide remains unexplored. And how should one read her departure from the bar following her "death"? The description of her leaving seems to be as much a beginning as an ending: "She passed the cluster of men at the bar and found herself again moving forward into the fiery red rays of the dying day" (p. 118). Moreover, the light of other sunsets playing on her child's face links this ending to the positive themes of freedom and escape (p. 64).

Many readers of *Moderato cantabile* are inclined to read Anne's fascination with the murder as her need for passion in a drab life of alienation. The murder, in this view, is remarkable for the emotional intensity it reveals, an intensity absent from Anne's conformist, bourgeois existence. Her "death" at the end of the novel is a kind of rebirth, a transformation wrought by the vicarious experience of great emotional intensity. Indeed, perhaps it is only the bourgeois married persona that has been "killed," leaving a new Anne revitalized by the experience.

Or perhaps one should not go too far in the direction of an optimistic, positive reading of the end of the novel. Perhaps the point of killing Anne in language only is that great passion is not so easily had in the modern world: only the simulacrum of passion, a futile and hollow gesture, is available to Anne and Chauvin.

Still other readings open new possibilities: one could reason, for example, that the crime serves as a warning to Anne, and that she thus manages to avoid the real violence that underlies her relationship with Chauvin and avoids becoming its victim.

None of these interpretations is wholly satisfying, however, in the sense that one possibility can be said to rule out the others, and most recent commentators avoid attempting a definitive reading of Anne's situation and motivation. As Leslie Hill observes,

From the outset, however, *Moderato cantabile* resists the imposition of any single frame of interpretation that would allow these dilemmas to be resolved. Various possibilities of reading co-exist in the text without any one version being privileged to the detriment of the others. Ambiguity and ambivalence are endemic; and like many of Duras's novels, the book is set in a world of blurred margins and uncertain border zones.[11]

Rather than attempt to resolve the ambiguity and ambivalence of *Moderato Cantabile*, many recent commentators see the ambiguity and ambivalence of desire as the very subject of the book. In doing so, they are recognizing the rather remarkable congruence between Duras's work and the psychoanalytic theories of Jacques Lacan. Such is this congruence that in 1965 Lacan proclaimed, regarding *The Ravishing of Lol Stein*, "[I]t turns out that Marguerite Duras knows, without me, what I teach."[12] Of the many aspects of Lacanian psychoanalysis that apply to Duras's books, the most useful in a discussion of *Moderato cantabile* is perhaps Lacan's understanding of desire.

In Freudian psychology, sexual wishes that are taboo, such as incestuous desires in childhood, are repressed and contained in the unconscious. What is to be done with such repressed desires is another question. In Freud's wake, various schools of thought have held that a repressive society is harmful, and that what is needed is a permissive society that would not render these sexual wants taboo; in such a society, liberated men and women would no longer feel alienated from their own sexuality. But for Lacan, the very nature of desire is inevitably bound up with the idea that it cannot be fully satisfied. Obviously, wants and needs can be met to some extent: a hungry child can eat, a longed-for absent person can return. But since the want or need first arose from some *absence, lack, or state of dissatisfaction,* the entire matter of satisfaction remains marked by an element of impossibility, as Juliet Mitchell explains:

Thus any satisfaction that might subsequently be attained will always contain this loss within it. Lacan refers to this dimension as "desire." The baby's needs can be met, its demand responded to, but its desire only exists because of the initial failure of satisfaction. Desire persists as an effect of a primordial absence and it therefore indicates that, in this area, there is something impossible about satisfaction itself.[13]

Such an understanding of desire goes a long way toward accounting for the otherwise curious atmosphere of *lack* in many of Duras's novels, and for many aspects of *Moderato cantabile*. From the inaugural event of the novel, the unnamed man's murder of his wife, it appears that desire is inextricably bound up with absence, in this case the absence of death:

The man lay down again beside his wife's body, but only for a moment. Then, as if he were tired, he got up again.
"Don't let him get away," the patronne shouted.
But the man had only got up in order to find a better position, closer to the body. He lay there, seemingly resolute and calm, holding her tightly in his arms, his face pressed to hers, in the blood flowing from her mouth. (p. 68)

The man's desire is expressed at the very moment that it cannot be realized, just as Anne and Chauvin's relationship seems to be brought into being as the function of its own impossibility. Thus their desire is enacted only in language, and the entire novel seems fundamentally based on alienation and absence.[14]

The Lover (1984)

Some of the success that The Lover enjoyed when it was published in 1984 stemmed from the public's fascination with the Duras persona and from the tendency of the book's first readers to treat it as autobiography. Set in the Indochina of Duras's youth, the book relates the love affair of a 15-year-old French girl, the daughter of an impoverished woman schoolteacher, and a 27-year-old Chinese man of a wealthy family. Some of the passages seem calculated to shock: "She says, I'd rather you didn't love me. But if you do, I'd like you to do as you usually do with women. He looks at her in horror, asks, Is that what you want? She says it is."[15] The story is told retrospectively by the girl as an adult and a writer; as Marilyn Schuster puts it, "The Lover was promoted as confessional literature: revelations about the scandalous interracial adolescent affair of a famous woman writer."[16] When Duras did an interview with Bernard Pivot for the well-known television show Apostrophes, Pivot discussed the book as though it were straightforwardly autobiographical.[17]

Indeed, it is very difficult not to read parts of the book as autobiography. Duras explained that the first impetus for the book was her examination of old family photographs,[18] and indeed many editions of The Lover have appeared with the portrait of the young Marguerite Donnadieu. For the reader with even the most passing familiarity with the adult Duras, passages such as the following have an immediately obvious connection with the author's life: "Now I see that when I was very young, eighteen, fifteen, I already had a face that foretold the one I acquired through drink in middle age" (pp. 8–9). Even the obvious dissimilarities between the book and Duras's life (for example, the girl in *The Lover* has two brothers whereas Duras had only one) do not entirely dispel one's first impression that there is a rather direct relationship between the events of the story and those of Duras's life. Nor did Duras do very much to forestall such speculation; she in fact encouraged this impression without ever confirming it.

Some observers have thought it an irony that the New Novelists, who preached and/or practiced a nonreferential literature, "the adventure of writing" rather than the "writing of an adventure," should turn to autobiography late in their careers. That they told their own real-life stories seems to demonstrate that vanity, if nothing else, finally brought these experimenters to their esthetic senses. "They all come to it. There's no avoiding it. Today, Duras; yesterday, Sartre, Ionesco, Barthes, Sarraute, Yourcenar; soon, Robbe-Grillet. They reject the cliché, 'autobiography.' Of course there's no linear narrative, no sincere confession to describe themselves as they are."[19] In the early 1980s, it did seem that they would all come to it. Nathalie Sarraute published *L'Enfance* (*Childhood*) in 1983; Robbe-Grillet's *Le Miroir qui revient* (*Ghosts in the Mirror*) appeared in 1984, the same year as *The Lover*. However, these *are* New Novelists, and the mere appearance of a text that looks like autobiography is no cause for celebration by traditionalists. *The Lover* in no sense represents a radical departure from what Duras was doing in books as early as *Moderato cantabile* and before.

When one gets well into *The Lover*, one discovers that the strong feeling one has that certain passages are autobiographical is not sustainable over the long run. It is not a matter of noticing factual discrepancies between the story and Duras's life; rather, the familiar themes of storytelling and blurring the distinction between life and narrative assert themselves again, as they do in *Moderato cantabile* and many of Duras's other works. The narrator of *The Lover* says:

The story of my life doesn't exist. Does not exist. There's never any center to it. No path, no line. There are great spaces where you pretend there used to be someone, but it's not true, there was no one. The story of one small part of my youth I've already written, more or less—I mean, enough to give a glimpse of it. Of this part, I mean, the part about the crossing of the river. What I'm doing now is both different and the same. (p. 8)

The feeling that writing is no direct conduit to lived experience is heightened by the discussion of photographs. While the photograph of the young Duras on the cover of the book adds a kind of authenticity to her fictional character's evocation of the past, it soon becomes apparent that the most central photograph, the one showing the 15-year-old narrator crossing the Mekong River on a ferry (at the end of the trip she will meet the man who is to become her lover), doesn't exist: "I think it was during this journey that the image became detached, removed from all the rest. It might have existed, a photograph might have been taken, just like any other, somewhere else, in other circumstances. But it wasn't. The subject was too slight" (p. 10). If photographs are taken to memorialize important occasions in life, it is only in retrospect that one knows what occasions are important: "The photograph could only have been taken if someone could have known in advance how important it was to be in my life, that event, the crossing of the river. But while it was happening, no one even knew of its existence. Except God. And that's why—it couldn't have been otherwise—the image doesn't exist. It was omitted. Forgotten" (p. 10). The blank space of the absent photograph is the site of writing, of representation and creation: "And it's to this, this failure to have been created, that the image owes its virtue: the virtue of representing, of being the creator of, an absolute" (p. 10). *The Lover* may be about Duras and in that sense autobiographical, but it is about Duras only by first being about writing, which makes the link between text and experience rather problematical: "The only subject of the book is writing," says Duras; "*I* am writing; therefore, I am the book."[20]

Another indication that we are in a space located somewhere between fiction and autobiography is the occasional intertextual reference to some of Duras's other works. For example, the character of Anne-Marie Stretter, from *The Ravishing of Lol Stein* and *The Vice-Consul*, appears as the Lady from Savanna Ket (p. 89). On the one hand, such an allusion to Duras's other books confirms the reader's suspicion that the young girl of *The Lover* who wants to be a writer is in fact a representation of the young Duras. But the other novels assert themselves in *The Lover* on the same plane as the events of the book; the young girl who has heard of the Lady from Savanna Ket is then both as fictional as Anne-Marie Stretter and as real as Marguerite Duras. Often Duras draws attention to her double stance toward fiction and autobiography in a single, short passage, as when she describes the car belonging to the man who is soon to be her lover: "On the ferry, beside the bus, there's a big black limousine with a chauffeur in white cotton livery. Yes, it's the big funereal car that's in my books. It's a Morris Léon-Bollée. The black Lancia at the French embassy in Calcutta [from *Le Vice-Consul*] hasn't yet made its entrance on the literary scene" (p. 17). The car has a reality outside books, but there is a strong reminder that we are watching a literary, that is, fictional, scene.

Thus the connection between writing and experience in *The Lover* is highly indeterminate; perhaps in recognition of this indeterminacy, Duras sometimes describes the girl's experiences in the first person and at other times refers to her character with the third-person "she."

As in *Moderato cantabile* and many other of Duras's books, a principal theme in *The Lover* is the relationship between a man and a woman. And while one cannot say that desire in *The Lover* is as disembodied as that of Anne Desbaresdes and Chauvin, because the young woman and her Chinese lover have a physical relationship that is described in detail, it is nevertheless true that the status of desire is quite as ambiguous as that of autobiography.

In this ambiguous space between autobiography and fiction, between memory and imagination, writing has a creative, determinative power. As the narrator reflects on the scene on the ferry, the scene that would have produced the photograph of a defining moment if anyone had thought to take it, her writing establishes certain things with a finality that memory cannot: "This particular day I must be wearing the famous pair of gold lamé high heels. I can't see any others I could have been wearing, so I'm wearing them" (p. 11). Just as the image of the girl on the ferry that is being shown to the reader is not determined by objective reality but is a projection of the writer, the girl understands that desire is principally an effect of mind. She "becomes" through desire in the same peremptory way that she declares that she was wearing the gold lamé shoes:

I know it's not a question of beauty, though, but of something else—mind, for example. What I want to seem, I do seem, beautiful too if that's what people want me to be. Beautiful or pretty, pretty for the family for example, for the family no more than that. I can become anything anyone wants me to be. And believe it. Believe I'm charming too. And when I believe it, and it becomes true for anyone seeing me who wants me to be according to his taste, I know that too. (p. 18)

In that sense, desire is an effect of mind but located in the person desired: "You didn't have to attract desire. Either it was in the woman who aroused it or it didn't exist. Either it was there at first glance or else it had never been. It was instant knowledge of sexual relationship or it was nothing. That too I knew before I experienced it" (p. 19).

The creation of desire takes place in both partners. When they make love for the first time, in a scene in which the girl rather perversely claims to feel no particular attachment to the man, she at first is aware of no real feelings: "She doesn't feel anything in particular, no hate, no repugnance either, so probably it's already desire. But she doesn't know it" (p. 36). Later in the same scene, her desire, born of his, is created, or revealed to her: "I notice that I desire him" (p. 40).

In Marilyn Schuster's analysis of the symbiotic play of desire in *The Lover*, the following is a key passage in which the transition to narrative is made explicit:

He looks at her. Goes on looking at her, his eyes shut. He inhales her face, breathes it in. He breathes her in, the child, his eyes shut he breathes in her breath, the warm air coming out of her. Less and less clearly can he make out the limits of this body, it's not like other bodies, it's not finished, in the room it keeps growing, it's still without set form, continually coming into being ... it launches itself wholly into pleasure as if it were grown up, adult, it's without guile, and it's frighteningly intelligent. (p. 99)

Schuster points out that since the lover's eyes are closed, he cannot be looking at the girl in any literal sense. Rather,

the lover's fantasy is the narrator's creation; she is imagining what he would have seen behind his closed eyes. The girl's body becomes powerful through his fantasy, but his fantasy is the invention of the narrator. The girl becomes a woman in a passage that ultimately reveals that the erotic is an invention of narrative.[21]

There are further revelations in this interactive play of desire and narrative at the end of *The Lover*. At the end of the narrated sequence of events, the girl sails to France on board a passenger liner. A suicide has taken place on the ship; a young man arose from his card game in the first-class bar and, without a word, threw himself over the side of the boat into the sea. The girl comes close to committing suicide herself, inexplicably, when the orchestra begins to play a Chopin waltz:

And the girl started up as if to go and kill herself in her turn, throw herself in her turn into the sea, and afterwards she wept because she thought of the man from Cholon [her lover] and suddenly she wasn't sure she hadn't loved him with a love she hadn't seen because it had lost itself in the affair like water in sand and she rediscovered it now, through this moment of music flung across the sea. (p. 114)

One is perhaps tempted to read the word "now" as the time of writing, with the written narrative being a kind of music "flung across the sea" to a lover from whom the narrator has long been separated. In any case, such a communication *does* take place at the end of the book, when the narrator recounts how, years later, her lover, now married to a proper Chinese wife, visits France and telephones her: "He phoned her. It's me. She recognized him at once from the voice. He said, I just wanted to hear your voice. She said, It's me, hello" (p. 116). The effect is of a dialogue that has never ceased, of a love affair, a desire that has been taking place in the very pages that narrate it. The last lines make this continuity very clear: "Then he didn't know what to say. And then he told her. Told her that it was as before, that he still loved her, he could never stop loving her, that he'd love her until death" (p. 117).

When Duras died in March 1996, articles in the American press reflected *The Lover's* importance in the public perception of her work. The *Los Angeles Times* headline was "Marguerite Duras; French Novelist wrote 'The Lover' "; the *New York Times* piece was entitled "Marguerite Duras, 81, Author Who Explored Love and Sex." Both articles discuss primarily *The Lover*, Duras's origins in Indochina, and the film made from the book in 1992. Neither piece mentions the New Novel.

But it should be apparent from the discussion here that there is a real continuity from *Moderato cantabile* through *The Lover*. One can argue that *The Lover's* huge success is due to the Duras public persona, the perceived confessional aspect of the work, or even its eroticism. The fact remains, however, that thousands of readers throughout the world read and enjoyed an innovative, elusive novel, and thousands more went to see a movie that, whatever the controversies between Duras and the director, attempted to translate into the film medium the book's "difficult" qualities as well as its erotic ones. Moreover, the book was read and enjoyed without engendering charges of unreadability, endless academic controversies, or apocalyptic claims of the Death of Literature. That this should be the case suggests, even bearing in mind that Duras never quite belonged to the movement, that at the end of the day we can conclude that the New Novel *succeeded*. It did not succeed in a way that any of the originators could have predicted: few of the readers of *The Lover* could begin to discuss any of the theories that went into the idea of the New Novel; most would be unable to name any of the other New Novelists. And it can hardly be said that the New Novel alone is responsible for the change. Even more tellingly, most readers of *The Lover*, even university students who discuss the book in a literature class, probably do not feel compelled to argue the "newness" of it as a novel. Nevertheless, the essential point of the New Novelists, that artistic forms evolve with other cultural changes, is proven.

8

Conclusion:
The Place of the New Novel

To situate the *nouveau roman* in the literary history of the twentieth century, one must first recognize that literary critics today apply to Western literature of the past hundred years the terms *modernism* and *postmodernism*, which were not in current usage when the concept of the New Novel was first formulated or even until the movement was somewhat past its prime. Although it is clear today that most of the New Novelists thought of themselves as the descendants of such modernist novelists as Dostoevsky, Proust, Joyce, Woolf, Faulkner, and Kafka, since the critical concepts that we now associate with modernism were not in place in the 1950s, the defining moment of the New Novel occurs mostly under the influence of existentialism and phenomenology. Indeed, from this perspective it would be tempting to think of the New Novel as a kind of "postexistentialist" literature. In many respects, the New Novelists appeared to be the existentialists' inheritors: Sartre wrote an influential preface for *Portrait d'un inconnu* and published Sarraute's articles in *Les Temps modernes;* Merleau-Ponty cited Simon's novels; and in American universities, the New Novel supplanted existentialism as the "hot" topic from Paris, at least until structuralism inherited that role a few years later. Existentialist literature was often the New Novelists' point of departure: Robbe-Grillet and, to a lesser extent, Sarraute wrote theoretical texts in which they interpreted the work of Sartre and Camus and defined themselves against these immediate predecessors.

Thus much of the early criticism of the New Novel approaches the subject from an existential or phenomenological point of view. In the 1960s and 1970s, the second phase of the New Novel and New Novel criticism and theory is structuralist in inspiration. By the time modernism and postmodernism became widely discussed and a poetics of modernist fiction was established, the cycles of academic fashion had brought the New Novel to a period of relative neglect, if only because so much attention had already been paid to

131

the phenomenon. It should be said, too, that while the notion of postmodernism was the subject of extremely lively debate in French circles owing mainly to Jean-François Lyotard's seminal work *The Postmodern Condition*, the idea of a literary *modernism* occurring in the first few decades of the twentieth century, as Fredric Jameson points out, came relatively late to French studies.[1] Why this should be the case is no doubt a complex question, but it might be noted that the modernist canon in France, which includes perhaps three writers of the first magnitude (Marcel Proust, André Gide, and Paul Valéry), is somewhat small when compared to modernist literature written in English.

Another factor that somewhat obscures the relationship between the New Novel and the modern/postmodern approach to literature is that a movement defined in the 1950s fell at an awkward time. There may be widely divergent opinions about the *beginning* of literary modernism (anywhere from 1850 until 1910), but nearly all observers place the *end* of the modernist period before World War II; 1955 is rather too late to launch a new wave of modernism. On the other hand, even though a post-World War II literary movement that adopts a revolutionary posture sounds rather postmodern, one would be slightly more comfortable situating the New Novel in respect to postmodernism if the New Novelists had begun writing 10 years or so *later* than they did. Moreover, any discussion of literature falling at the end of the modernist period, or between modernism and postmodernism, is complicated by a theoretical question that for a while dominated discussions of postmodernism: is postmodernism primarily a development of modernism, or a more radical break with what went before?[2] Where one situates the New Novel depends to some extent on how one answers this question.

Despite these difficulties, it is worthwhile to attempt to understand the significance of the New Novel in terms of modernism and postmodernism, particularly if one understands that the point is not so much to decide which label to apply to the New Novel and its various practitioners but rather to use the conceptual tools of cultural criticism to illuminate key aspects of these works, and to read them against the broader movements of French and European culture. Indeed, it would be wise to anticipate finding elements of both modernism and postmodernism in the New Novel, given that many of the critics who have discussed the New Novel in these terms have come to rather different conclusions. Certain observers, such as Morton Levitt, argue for the New Novel as a continuation of modernism, whereas others, for example John Calder, take the view that these novels are fundamentally postmodern.[3]

Perhaps the most fundamental element of modernism is the individual's conviction that he or she is engaged in the process of historical change: the realities of one's situation have not always been as they are now, nor will they stay the same in the future. Similarly, one may expect that ways of understanding those realities will not remain the same from one era to the next. The origin of this sense of historical relativism lies in the great shift in European civilization in the Renaissance known as modernity, but by the beginning of the twentieth century, two further conditions obtained. First, historical relativism appeared to many to be natural and acceptable rather an idea to be struggled against. Second, by this time the notion of relativism had finally been extended to aesthetics; since the Romantic period of the early nineteenth century, each age has had the right to establish its own standards of beauty rather than imitate classical antiquity's eternal standards of beauty.

With respect to this historical relativism, it is clear that at the beginning of its history in the 1950s the New Novel was squarely within the modernist tradition. Robbe-Grillet's main argument, that Balzac wrote novels that may have been appropriate to the world view of French culture in 1830 but that cannot hope to suit the reader of 1955, is exactly the sort of cultural relativism that characterizes the modernist spirit: "to write like Stendhal one would first of all have to be writing in 1830."[4] The error of those who are opposed to the New Novel, in Robbe-Grillet's opinion, is to elevate Balzac's novelistic practice to the status of an absolute standard for fiction writing when in fact it succeeded only because it was suited, in relativistic fashion, to the ideology of a particular time and place. It is significant that most of Robbe-Grillet's arguments are directed against the realist novel of the first half of the nineteenth century and certain of its techniques; the modernist novelists were rebelling against the same conception of the novel, and in many respects Robbe-Grillet's "revolution" sounds like a continuation of the modernists'. In effect, Robbe-Grillet's was the last argument in the quarrel of the ancients and moderns, dating from the sixteenth century, in which was debated the right of each age to establish its own taste. Those of the New Novelists who wrote theoretical texts during the first phase of the New Novel—Robbe-Grillet, Sarraute, and Butor—

are unanimous in their relativistic opinion that Balzac was the "New Novelist" of 1830, Flaubert of 1857, Joyce of 1920, and so on. If they claim to write the New Novels of 1955, it is with no pretension that they and not others have at long last discovered the best way to write novels: someone else will write the New Novels of 1975, 2000, and so on. Literature, like everything else, makes progress.[5] Their attitude is that the novel is an inexhaustible genre, and one should revel in the endless possibilities it presents.

Another piece of evidence that the first phase of the New Novel is primarily modernist in character is the self-conscious interest that many of these novelists had in questions of technique. One of the most striking signs of the change from the realist novels of the first half of the nineteenth century to modernist fiction is a change in narration from the "omniscient" practices of Balzac or Dickens, in which an impersonal narrator tells the story from a godlike vantage point, to point-of-view narrative techniques described by Henry James and virtually promoted to the status of doctrine in the first half of this century. The French narrative theorist Gérard Genette provides a new narrative taxonomy that is helpful in this context, using the optical metaphor "focalization" to describe the relation between the narration and the events of which it is composed.[6] "Focalization" means "restriction of field"; thus a focalized narrative is one that presents its story from a relativistic, restricted vantage point. Internal focalization locates this vantage point in the consciousness of a particular character and produces a narrative that lets the reader witness and know only what the character can witness and know. External focalization locates the narrative vantage point outside all the characters, as though the narrative were the verbal product, so to speak, of a movie camera: the reader knows *less* than the characters know. A nonfocalized narrative ("omniscient," in the traditional vocabulary) suffers no restrictions, and the reader knows *more* than the characters can realistically know.

This change in narrative technique from nonfocalized to focalized is reckoned to arise from a pervasive feeling among modernists that an established order had collapsed and that any attempt to recover order must be made on the individual level. The realist novel supposes shared values and a common understanding of the world between author and reader, whereas the modernist believes that values, even truth, depend on individual experience. As the British novelist Anthony Trollope put it, making explicit the implicit pact between the realist author and his or her readers, "Our doctrine is, that the author and the reader should move along together in full confidence with each other."[7] The modernist position was first articulated by Henry James: "[A man] and his neighbors are watching the same show, but one seeing more where the other sees less, one seeing black where the other sees white, one seeing big where the other sees small, one seeing coarse where the other sees fine."[8]

Writing about James Joyce's *A Portrait of the Artist as a Young Man*, Morton Levitt shows how modernist narration is connected to the modernist world view:

> Thrust without warning into a consciousness which cannot order the events that it observes, which is incapable of distinguishing among levels of truth or even of sorting out its own sensory perceptions, the reader understands at once that he is in a new world, with changing forces and shifting boundaries, with none of the certainty that Trollope desires and that he himself has long been accustomed to.[9]

This passage could be applied, almost word for word, to any number of New Novels, *The Flanders Road*, for instance. The first half of it at least could also be used to describe the phenomenological view of consciousness, in which consciousness confronts the world without preexisting ordering notions. These convergences show that there are certain commonalities to modernism, phenomenology, and the New Novel. That the New Novel, once described as "phenomenological," should now be called "modernist" is not at all contradictory; indeed, the terms *phenomenology* and *modernism*, applied to fiction, seem in many important respects to be different ways of arriving at quite similar conclusions.

Many New Novels, particularly during the first phase, can strike the reader as experiments in narrative technique by authors who think of narrative point of view as an important aspect of the novel. *Jealousy* in particular seems concerned with testing the limits of internal focalization, and surely one of the processes of discovery the reader is intended to go through is to realize what a truly radical subjective narrative might look like. *A Change of Heart*, too, seems self-consciously to make a statement about narrative technique by adopting the *other* personal pronoun, the second, not much used in a genre that in its history seemed to be enraptured initially with the third person, then with the first. Nathalie Sarraute and the early Claude Simon do not perhaps give the same impression of being interested in technique for the sake of technique; with them, the point is how technique can best serve a particular vision of human psychology. Nevertheless, narrative perspective is important to their fictional worlds and is a notable feature of most of their novels.

Beyond the New Novel's first phase, however, it is much less tempting to associate the New Novel with systematic experimentation in narrative technique. Formal innovation and experimentation continue, of course, but over a broad spectrum of aspects of the novel. Robbe-Grillet's later novels certainly continue to work self-consciously with novelistic form, but *Djinn*, for example, has little to do with the modernists' technical preoccupations. Simon's critique of representation in *Triptych* and others of his later novels has little of strictly narrative significance, Butor stops writing narratives altogether, and Duras seems never to have been interested in deliberately playing with narrative perspective.

In many other ways as well, the later New Novels are less reminiscent of modernist ones. In contrast to modernism's sense of the progressive unfolding of history, the postmodern age is marked, as Fredric Jameson puts it, by "senses of the end of this or that (the end of ideology, art, or social class; the 'crisis' of Leninism, social democracy, or the welfare state, etc., etc.); taken together, all of these perhaps constitute what is increasingly called postmodernism."[10] One of the key essays in the definition of a postmodern literature is "The Literature of Exhaustion," by the American novelist John Barth. This essay was written in 1967, only four years after the publication of Robbe-Grillet's *For a New Novel*, but it is very different from that work in argument and in tone. In the first place, Barth sees the question facing novelists to be that of going beyond the modernists, not the realists. In the second, it isn't clear to him that the novel can really go anywhere, in the modernist sense of "progress": "By 'exhaustion' I don't mean anything so tired as the subject of physical, moral, or intellectual decadence, only the used-upness of certain forms or the felt exhaustion of certain possibilities—by no means necessarily a cause for despair."[11] This view of literature is historical, like the modernist view, but it is not the same sort of history. The modernists' history is progressive, an ongoing search for new forms, new values, and new truths; the notion that this search may have reached an end, whether successful in the sense of finding an absolute truth or unsuccessful, is foreign to their thinking. The spirit that Barth describes is aware of history but lacks the modernist view of history as an essentially endless process of change. In postmodernism, pastiche of older forms in the "retro" mode is often the form taken by historical awareness.

Yet Barth's "exhaustion" should not be confused with despair or sterility, for the postmodern notion of history still allows for productivity, if not exactly innovation and originality. His example is the famous story by Argentinian writer Jorge Luis Borges, "Pierre Menard, Author of the Quixote," in which a fin-de-siècle French writer recomposes, word for word, Cervantes's novel. Of course any modernist would understand that a text produced in seventeenth-century Spain would not have the same effect, the same meaning, if it were written in late-nineteenth-century France, but Borges makes this point with considerable irony:

> It is a revelation to compare Menard's *Don Quixote* with Cervantes's. The latter, for example, wrote (part one, chapter nine): ". . . truth, whose mother is history, rival of time, depository of deeds, witness of the past, exemplar and adviser to the present, the future's counselor." Written in the seventeenth century, written by the "lay genius" Cervantes, this enumeration is a mere rhetorical praise of history. Menard, on the other hand, writes: ". . . truth, whose mother is history, rival of time, depository of deeds, witness of the past, exemplar and adviser to the present, the future's counselor." History, the *mother* of truth: the idea is astounding. Menard, a contemporary of William James, does not define history as an inquiry into reality but as its origin.[12]

Barth sees in this play not futility but an important commentary on art:

> Borges *doesn't* attribute the *Quixote* to himself, much less recompose it like Pierre Menard; instead, he writes a remarkable and original work of literature, the implicit theme of which is the difficulty, perhaps the unnecessity, of writing original works of literature. His artistic victory, if you like, is that he confronts an intellectual dead end and employs it against itself to accomplish a new human work.[13]

The New Novel certainly provides instances of the kind of play that Borges engages in: one thinks first of Robbe-Grillet's works, and a novel like Simon's *Triptych* is quite as paradoxical, if perhaps not as droll, as the story of Pierre Menard. What is not evident in the early years of the New Novel, however, is Barth's sense of "the used-upness of certain forms." In their theoretical texts and interviews of the 1950s, the New Novelists' main argument is for a new *kind* of literature, a renewal of the novel through formal innovation, and one senses that the aim of much of the self-conscious play in the early New Novel is to undermine a certain literary tradition without calling into question the notion of literature itself.

The second phase of the New Novel, in the late 1960s and the 1970s, produced both novels and commentary that seem much more connected to postmodernism than do the works of the first phase. Whereas the modernist view of literary history is one of never-ending development, with new techniques being devised to represent new realities, the structuralist attack on literary representation seems at times to announce an end to all that and to remind one of John Barth's sense of the "used-upness of certain forms." A typical comment of Robbe-Grillet from this period is the following, from a television appearance: "[The novelist] speaks, and at the same time nothing remains of what he says since everything is destroyed as he speaks it, as though the only interesting thing were the movement of language, and not at all of what it says; it is the creative movement of a language that believes in nothing apart from what it is saying at the moment."[14] Certain of Claude Simon's pronouncements have an air of postmodern bleakness about them too: "Everything means nothing, and ultimately there is nothing to say," although there is perhaps in such sentiments more exhaustion than exhausted possibilities, to return to Barth's useful distinction.

Thus representation is eliminated from the novel, leaving only the process of signifying, rather than the thing that is finally signified. This endlessly indeterminate play of meaning is another feature of postmodernism, as Ernst Behler writes:

[T]he relationship between signifier and signified is no longer intact, in that signs do not refer to something signified, a pregiven entity, but always to other signs. We thus never reach the true meaning of things, but only other signs, interpretations of other signs, interpretations of interpretations, and we move along in an endless chain of signification.[15]

Behler's metaphor of an endless chain of signification seems an apt way of describing Simon's *Triptych*, in which one goes from one mode of representation to another without ever finding anything that can be called more "real" than everything else. Robbe-Grillet's *Djinn* comes to mind, too, with its story partly determined by the sequencing of grammar items in a foreign-language textbook.

In *Metafiction: The Theory and Practice of Self-Conscious Fiction,* Patricia Waugh suggests an interesting distinction between modern and postmodern ways in which the novel can be about itself.[16] The reflexivity of the modernist novel is typically on the creative consciousness, whereas postmodern fictionality is a laying bare of the constitutive structures of fiction itself. Although Waugh is the first to concede that such a broad distinction cannot be applied in every case, her observation permits one to see the difference between certain of the New Novelists' practices. Such novels as Sarraute's *Between Life and Death,* Butor's *A Change of Heart,* and Simon's *The Flanders Road* all have metafictional elements that point more toward the functioning of the creative consciousness than toward the artifacts of fiction itself, and in that sense they may be associated more with modernism (or phenomenology) than with postmodernism. Simon's *Triptych* and Robbe-Grillet's *Djinn,* on the other hand, draw the reader's attention to questions of fiction making and representation rather than to the consciousness behind such representation and are thus reflexive in a postmodern way. Indeed, even Robbe-Grillet's early fiction seems to contain a self-conscious play about the structures of fiction itself, and so the argument can be made that in his fictional practice, at least, Robbe-Grillet showed early signs of postmodern sensibility, although much of his early theorizing has a decidedly modern cast.

Waugh recognizes, however, that no neat boundaries can be drawn in this way. To say, for example, that postmodern metafiction consists in laying bare the conventions of fiction suggests that much eighteenth-century metafiction, such as Sterne's *Tristram Shandy* or Diderot's *Ceci n'est pas un conte* (*This is not a Story*), is postmodern, which does not make very much sense.[17]

Indeed, there is little sense in attempting do define *any* novelistic technique as postmodern, since one of the hallmarks of the postmodern age is a multiplicity of heterogeneous techniques. The postmodern attitude toward art is one of "used-up" forms that are, paradoxically, continually revisited, in historical but nonprogressive moves. The idea that the history of an artistic form is advanced in broad, innovative changes, such as a shift in narrative perspective, is modernist, not postmodern.

To take this argument a step further, a movement such as the New Novel that may be said to possess a central argument about the novel cannot really be said to be postmodern. The cohesiveness of the New Novel group has always been a subject of debate, but one can add to the debate the observation that to the extent that the New Novel *is* cohesive, it is modernist. If it is true as argued here that one begins to see more and more postmodern elements in the later stages of the New Novel, it is also true, and not coincidentally, that in those later stages of development it becomes increasingly harder to speak of "a" New Novel at all. Indeed, "postmodern*ism*" is almost a contradiction in terms, for the present condition of cultural production is not at all conducive to "isms" of any kind; Morton Levitt observes that the late twentieth century is "a literary age in process of formation, more likely a series of separate movements (most of them so individualistic and specialized that they should perhaps be called 'moves' rather than 'movements' and the whole labeled 'gestures' rather than an 'age'); an age whose attributes are perceived primarily in terms of what it is not."[18] In this respect, Marguerite Duras, who was never at ease as part of the New Novel and who is surely aware of her novelistic predecessors but never preoccupied with them, who is little inclined to theory and in whose novels technique seems beside the point, is perhaps the most truly postmodern of all the New Novelists. Or one might think of Claude Simon, not really a theorist but nevertheless issuing diverse theoretical statements among which he moves so freely as to discount the notion of theory altogether.[19]

The New Novel occupies an intriguing position in the literary history of the twentieth century. Composed of writers who at times seemed very different from one another, the movement may be thought of as a set of links between certain elements: between modernism and postmodernism, for example, or between existentialism and structuralism. Perhaps the best way to sum up the New Novel is to say that it was the *last* literary movement; there were other "isms" still to come in France, structuralism and poststructuralism, as well as a variety of feminisms, but these were and are theoretical discourses rather than literary ones.[20] If the theoretical statements of the New Novel sometimes have a faintly archaic sound to them, it is because the age of literary movements is past.

Notes and References

CHAPTER 1

1. *Esprit* 7–8 (July-August 1958).

2. Maurice Nadeau, "Nouvelles formules pour le roman," *Critique* 13, nos. 123–24 (August-September 1957): 707–22. The phrase "nouveau roman" appears to be an editorial addition: on the cover, it appears as the title of Nadeau's article, and it is the title that appears as a running header, but the title in the table of contents and on the first page of the article is "Nouvelles formules pour le roman." See also Gerald Prince, "The Nouveau roman," in *A New History of French Literature*, ed. Denis Hollier (Cambridge: Harvard University Press, 1989), 989.

3. *Yale French Studies* 24 (1959).

4. Roland Barthes, "Littérature objective," *Critique* 10, nos. 86–87 (July-August 1954): 581–91.

5. John Sturrock, *The French New Novel: Claude Simon, Michel Butor, Alain Robbe-Grillet* (London: Oxford University Press, 1969), 1.

6. Pierre de Boisdeffre, *La Cafetière est sur la table ou contre le "nouveau roman"* (Paris: La Table ronde de combat, 1967), 147–50. My translation.

7. Truman Capote, "The $6 Misunderstanding," *New York Review of Books* 1, no. 2 (1963): 14.

8. Régis Debray, *Teachers, Writers, Celebrities: The Intellectuals of Modern France*, trans. David Macey (London: NLB, 1981), 56.

9. Leon S. Roudiez, *French Fiction Today: A New Direction* (New Brunswick, New Jersey: Rutgers University Press, 1972), 6.

10. Morton P. Levitt, *Modernist Survivors* (Columbus: Ohio State University Press, 1987), 124.

11. Especially useful discussions of the phenomenological and structuralist New Novel are found in David Carroll, *The Subject in Question: The Languages of Theory and the Strategies of Fiction* (Chicago: The University of Chicago Press, 1982), 9–26, and in Celia Britton, *Claude Simon: Writing the Visible* (Cambridge: Cambridge University Press, 1987), 1–17.

12. Carroll, *The Subject in Question*, 9.

13. Nicole Aas-Rouxparis, "L'Evolution du roman: Interview de Claude Ollier," *Letteratura Francese Contemporanea* 4, no. 8 (July 1983): 155–60. My translation.

CHAPTER 2

1. Alain Robbe-Grillet, *For a New Novel: Essays on Fiction*, trans. Richard Howard (New York: Grove Press, 1965), 9; hereafter cited in the text.

2. See, for example, Eric Gans, "The Last French Novels," *Romanic Review* 83, no. 4 (November 1992): 500–516, and Levitt, *Modernist Survivors*.

3. Jonathan Culler, *Roland Barthes* (New York: Oxford University Press, 1983), 54–55.

4. Robbe-Grillet, *The Erasers*, trans. Richard Howard (New York: Grove Press, 1964), 152–53.

5. Jean-Paul Sartre, "Explication de 'L'Etranger,'" *Situations* I (Paris: Gallimard, 1947), 92–112.

6. Albert Camus, *Le Mythe de Sisyphe* (Paris: Gallimard-Folio, 1985), 39.

7. Sartre, *La Nausée* (Paris: Gallimard-Folio, 1988), 13; my translation.

8. Roland Barthes, *Critical Essays*, trans. Richard Howard (Evanston: Northwestern University Press, 1972), 14.

9. Sartre, *Nausea*, trans. Lloyd Alexander (New York: New Directions, 1964) 130–31.

10. Sartre, *Nausea*, 131.

11. Robbe-Grillet, *Jealousy: A Novel*, trans. Richard Howard (New York: Grove Press, 1959), 51.

12. Barthes, "The Last Word on Robbe-Grillet?," in *Critical Essays*, 198; Stephen Heath, *The Nouveau roman: A Study in the Practice of Writing* (Philadelphia: Temple University Press, 1972), 67.

13. See, for example, Philippe Sollers's review of *Pour un nouveau roman* in *Tel Quel*, no. 18 (Summer 1964): 93–94.

14. Bruce Morrissette, *Les Romans de Robbe-Grillet* (Paris: Editions de Minuit, 1971), 28–29.

15. Ibid., 29.

16. Heath, *The Nouveau roman*, 85.

17. Maurice Merleau-Ponty, *Phénoménologie de la perception* (Paris: Gallimard, 1945), v. Quoted in Heath, *The Nouveau roman*, 92. My translation.

18. Madeleine Chapsal, *Les Ecrivains en personne* (Paris: Julliard, 1960), 215. Quoted in Heath, *The Nouveau roman*, 86. My translation.

19. Merleau-Ponty, *Phénoménologie de la perception*, 83. Quoted in Heath, *The Nouveau roman*, 97. My translation.

20. Interview in *Les Nouvelles littéraires* (5 February 1970): 2. Quoted by Heath, *The Nouveau roman*, 115n. My translation.

21. Lois Oppenheim, ed., *Three Decades of the French New Novel* (Urbana: University of Illinois Press, 1986), 25–26. See also Morrissette, *Les Romans de Robbe-Grillet*, 21.

22. *Larousse Dictionary of Writers*, ed. Rosemary Goring (Edinburgh: Larousse, 1994), 820.

23. Thomas Frick, review of *La Belle captive* in the *Los Angeles Times Book Review* (14 May 1995): 6.

24. Ferdinand de Saussure, *Course in General Linguistics*, trans. Wade Baskin (New York: The Philosophical Library, 1959), 121.

25. Jean Ricardou, ed., *Robbe-Grillet: Colloque de Cerisy* (Paris: Union Générale d'Editions, 1976) I, 29.

26. Robbe-Grillet, *Jealousy*, 127.

27. Ricardou, ed., *Robbe-Grillet: Colloque de Cerisy* I, 16. My translation.

28. Ibid., 40.

29. Nathalie Sarraute, *The Age of Suspicion: Essays on the Novel*, trans. Maria Jolas (New York: George Braziller, 1963), 71; hereafter cited in the text.

30. Sarraute uses the French word *mouvements,* translated as "movements" in the English translations of her works. Vivian Mercier, in *The New Novel, from Queneau to Pinget* (New York: Farrar, Strauss and Giroux, 1971), 104, points out that the French word can also, and more plausibly in this context, be translated as "emotions" or "emotional stirrings."

31. Sarraute, *Tropisms,* trans. Maria Jolas (New York: George Braziller, n.d.), vi.

32. Over the author's objections, however: Sarraute has often rejected comparisons of her work and Woolf's. See Ruby Cohn, "Nathalie Sarraute et Virginia Woolf," in *Revue des Lettres Modernes,* nos. 94–99 (1964).

33. Oppenheim, ed., *Three Decades of the French New Novel,* 28.

CHAPTER 3

1. François Jost makes light of this commonplace by calling them the "Scylla and Charybdis" of French letters in "Petit dictionnaire des idées reçues sur Alain Robbe-Grillet," *Obliques* 16/17 (1978): 264.

2. Culler, *Roland Barthes* , 54.

3. Roland Barthes, "Objective Literature," in *Critical Essays,* 13–24.

4. Published by the publisher of Robbe-Grillet's novels, Les Editions de Minuit, which employed Robbe-Grillet as editorial consultant at the time. When one adds that the journal *Critique,* where Barthes's early articles on Robbe-Grillet appeared, was published by Minuit, it becomes apparent that the world of Robbe-Grillet studies was small indeed.

5. Morrissette, *Les Romans de Robbe-Grillet,* 39n.

6. Morrissette, *The Novels of Robbe-Grillet* (Ithaca: Cornell University Press, 1975), 53.

7. Morrissette, *Les Romans de Robbe-Grillet,* 53n.

8. Morrissette, *The Novels of Robbe-Grillet,* 64.

9. Ibid., 65–66.

10. Ibid., 69.

11. Barthes, "The Last Word on Robbe-Grillet?" in *Critical Essays,* 197–204.

12. Ibid., 198.

13. Ibid., 201.

14. Ibid., 200.

15. Ibid., 202.

16. Olga Bernal, *Alain Robbe-Grillet: le roman de l'absence* (Paris: Gallimard, 1964), 60–61.

17. Leon S. Roudiez, *French Fiction Today: A New Direction* (New Brunswick, New Jersey: Rutgers University Press, 1972), 209.

18. Heath, *The Nouveau roman,* 67.

19. Ilona Leki, *Alain Robbe-Grillet* (Boston: Twayne, 1983), 5. Many years after *Jealousy,* when he was interested in the autobiographical nature of creative fiction, Robbe-Grillet revealed casually that the story of *Jealousy* as well as its locale was based on real events, with Robbe-Grillet in the role of Franck. Whether the husband's jealousy was justified or not remains a

mystery, however! See Jean-Jacques Brochier, interview of Alain Robbe-Grillet in *Magazine littéraire* 250 (February 1988): 90–97.

20. I am modifying many of Richard Howard's translations in this section.

21. Robbe-Grillet once declared that he deliberately made it impossible to reconstruct the chronology of *La Jalousie*.

22. Bruce Morrissette, *Intertextual Assemblages in Robbe-Grillet from Topology to the Golden Triangle* (Fredericton, New Brunswick: York Press, 1979).

23. Alain Robbe-Grillet, *Djinn*, trans. Yvone Lenard and Walter Wells (New York: Grove Press, 1987), 7–10; hereafter cited in the text.

24. Heath, *The Nouveau roman*, 70.

25. Robbe-Grillet, *Ghosts in the Mirror*, trans. Jo Levy (New York: Grove Weidenfeld, 1984), 169. This idea that the ideology in his books is not his own but merely what he finds floating about him in society is Robbe-Grillet's answer to the charge that many of his works revolve around sadoerotic violence. If women are victims in his books, it is because those books parody the victimization of women as it exists in male fantasies. The argument is not entirely convincing.

26. Robbe-Grillet, "Pourquoi j'aime Barthes," in *Prétexte: Roland Barthes*, ed. Antoine Compagnon (Paris: Union Générale d'Editions, 1978). My translation.

CHAPTER 4

1. I follow here Sarraute's own account of her early career published in Oppenheim, ed., *Three Decades of the French New Novel*, 119–31.

2. Alain Robbe-Grillet, "Le réalisme, la psychologie, et l'avenir du roman," *Critique* 111–12 (August-September 1956): 695–701.

3. Nathalie Sarraute, *Portrait of a Man Unknown*, trans. Maria Jolas (New York: George Braziller, 1958), 17–18; hereafter cited in the text.

4. Sartre, *Nausea*, 66–67. Translation modified.

5. Sarraute, "Tolstoi," *Les lettres françaises* 22 (September 1960): 7. Quoted in Sheila M. Bell, *Nathalie Sarraute: "Portrait d'un inconnu" and "Vous les entendez?"* (London: Grant and Cutler, Critical Guides to French Texts, 1988), 26. My translation.

6. For a different view that sees the narrator as inauthentic, see Micheline Tison Braun, *Nathalie Sarraute ou la Recherche de l'authenticité* (Paris: Gallimard, 1971).

7. Sartre, *Les Ecrivains en personne*, ed. M. Chapal (Paris: 1960), 213–14. Quoted by Heath, *The Nouveau roman*, 57. My translation.

8. See Heath, *The Nouveau roman*, 54–58; Vivian Mercier, *The New Novel*, 143.

9. Mary McCarthy, "Hanging by a Thread," in *The Writing on the Wall and Other Literary Essays* (New York: Harcourt, Brace & World, 1970), 183.

10. Heath, *The Nouveau roman*, 60.

11. Hérault is the name of a French department; héraut means "herald"; "héros" is "hero"; "aire haut" is something like "lofty area"; "erre

haut" is "wanders aloft"; "R.O." are letters of the alphabet that rhyme with the other words in this series.

12. Oppenheim, ed., *Three Decades of the French New Novel*, 10.

13. Quoted in Bell, *Nathalie Sarraute: "Portrait d'un inconnu" and "Vous les entendez?"*, 16. My translation.

14. Oppenheim, ed., *Three Decades of the French New Novel*, 122. My translation.

15. Sarraute, *L'Ere du soupçon* (Paris: Gallimard Idées, 1964), 12. My translation.

CHAPTER 5

1. Butor, *Essais sur le roman* (Paris: Gallimard, 1969), 15.

2. I discuss here ideas expressed primarily in Butor, "Research on the Technique of the Novel" and "The Novel as Research," in *Inventory: Essays by Michel Butor*, ed. Richard Howard (New York: Simon and Schuster, 1968), 15–30; hereafter cited in the text.

3. Notable discussions of the phenomenological interest of *La Modification* may be found in Lois Oppenheim, *Intentionality and Intersubjectivity: A Phenomenological Study of Butor's* La Modification (Lexington, Kentucky: French Forum, Publishers, 1980), and in Jean H. Duffy, *Butor:* La Modification (London: Grant & Cutler, 1990).

4. Butor, "Balzac and Reality," in *Inventory*, ed. Richard Howard, 100; hereafter cited in the text. This is one of Butor's articles on the novel that is not published in *Essais sur le roman*.

5. Butor, *A Change of Heart*, trans. Jean Stewart (New York: Simon and Schuster, 1959), 1; hereafter cited in the text.

6. Butor, "L'usage des pronoms personnels dans le roman," in *Essais sur le roman*, 73–88. My translation.

7. Mary Lydon, *Perpetuum Mobile: A Study of the Novels and Aesthetics of Michel Butor* (Edmonton: University of Alberta Press, 1980), 100.

8. Butor, *Le Génie du lieu*, quoted in Dean McWilliams, *The Narratives of Michel Butor: The Writer as Janus* (Ohio University Press, 1978), 36.

9. Mercier, *The New Novel*, 219.

10. Quoted in Lydon, *Perpetuum Mobile*, 103. My translation.

11. Jean Renaudot, "Parenthèse sur la place occupée par l'étude intitulée '6 810 000 litres d'eau par seconde' parmi les autres ouvrages de Michel Butor," *Nouvelle Revue Française* 165 (September 1966): 498–509; quoted in Roudiez, *French Fiction Today*, 293.

12. In *Inventory*, ed. Richard Howard, 39–56.

13. *Niagara: a Novel by Michel Butor*, trans. Elinor S. Miller (Chicago: Henry Regnery Company, 1969), 2; hereafter cited in the text.

14. See Friedrich Nietzsche, *Twilight of the Idols*, in *The Portable Nietzsche*, ed. and trans. Walter Kaufmann (New York: Penguin Books, 1959), 480.

15. Butor, "Chateaubriand and Early America," in *Inventory*, ed. Richard Howard, 59–99.

16. McWilliams, *The Narratives of Michel Butor*, 79.

17. *Inventory*, ed. Richard Howard, 25.

CHAPTER 6

1. Angelo Rinaldi in *L'Express* (1 November 1985), quoted in Madeleine Raaphorst-Rousseau, "L'Année littéraire 1985," *The French Review* 59, no. 1 (May 1986): 952 (my translation); "Letter from Paris," *Vogue* (January 1986): 102ff.

2. *Time* (28 October 1985): 88.

3. *Los Angeles Times* (18 October 1985): 16.

4. John Fletcher, *Claude Simon and Fiction Now* (London: Calder and Boyars, 1975); J. A. E. Loubère, *The Novels of Claude Simon* (Ithaca: Cornell University Press, 1975); Salvador Jimènez-Fajardo, *Claude Simon*: (Boston: Twayne, 1975). By 1975, in contrast, the number of books exclusively on Robbe-Grillet was in the double digits.

5. Jacques Guicharnaud, "Remembrance of Things Passing: Claude Simon," in *Yale French Studies* 24 (1959): 101–8.

6. For example, Celia Britton, *Claude Simon: Writing the Visible* (Cambridge: Cambridge University Press, 1987); David Carroll, *The Subject in Question: The Languages of Theory and the Strategies of Fiction* (Chicago: University of Chicago Press, 1982); Lucien Dällenbach, *Claude Simon* (Paris: Seuil, 1988); Ralph Sarkonak, *Claude Simon: les carrefours du texte* (Toronto: Editions Paratexte, 1986).

7. See Loubère, *The Novels of Claude Simon*, 46–59 for a survey of these novels.

8. Fletcher, introduction, in Claude Simon, *The Flanders Road*, trans. Richard Howard (London: John Calder, 1985), 4. Quotations from the novel are taken from this edition, henceforth cited in the text.

9. Quoted by Lucien Dällenbach, "Le Tissu de mémoire," in *La Route des Flandres* (Paris: Editions de Minuit, 1982), 300–301. Originally published in *Le Monde* 8 (October 1960). My translation.

10. Lucien Dällenbach, "Le Tissu de mémoire," 302.

11. See Jean Duffy, "Claude Simon, Merleau-Ponty and Perception," in *French Studies* 46, no. 1 (1992): 33–52.

12. Quoted in Duffy, "Claude Simon, Merleau-Ponty and Perception," 35. My translation.

13. Interview of Claude Simon by Aliette Armel in *Magazine littéraire* 275 (March 1990): 100.

14. The original of this portrait hangs in Claude Simon's home in Roussillon. See Loubère, *The Novels of Claude Simon*, 90n.

15. Maurice Merleau-Ponty, "Cinq notes sur Claude Simon," *Méditations* 4 (Winter 1961–1962): 5–9. Quoted in Loubère, *The Novels of Claude Simon*, 99.

16. Quoted in Duffy, "Claude Simon, Merleau-Ponty and Perception," 37.

17. Quoted in Mercier, *The New Novel*, 268. Mercier's translation.

18. Loubère, *The Novels of Claude Simon*, 93.

19. Heath, *The Nouveau roman*, 166.

20. Loubère, *The Novels of Claude Simon*, 86.

21. Ricardou, "La Littérature comme critique," excerpted in *Les critiques de notre temps et le nouveau roman*, ed. Réal Ouellet (Paris: Garnier, 1972), 22.

22. Claude Simon, *Orion aveugle* (Geneva: Skira, 1970), 5. My translation.

23. Interview of Claude Simon by Aliette Armel, 101.

24. Quoted in Duffy, "Claude Simon, Merleau-Ponty, and Perception," 35.

25. Simon, *Triptych*, trans. Helen R. Lane (New York: Viking, 1976), 1; henceforth cited in the text.

26. Simon, *Orion aveugle*, 11–12. My translation.

CHAPTER 7

1. See, for example, Armand Hoog's article on Duras in the "Midnight Novelists" issue of *Yale French Studies*, 68–73: "She is a great novelist who will rise superior to the perils of the literary 'school.' "

2. Elaine Marks and Isabelle de Courtivron, eds., *New French Feminisms: An Anthology* (New York: Schocken, 1981), 174.

3. Marks and de Courtivron, eds., *New French Feminisms*, 111.

4. Marguerite Duras and Xavière Gauthier, *Woman to Woman*, trans. Katharine A. Jensen (Lincoln: University of Nebraska Press, 1987), 145.

5. Marilyn R. Schuster, *Marguerite Duras Revisited* (New York: Twayne, 1993), x.

6. Germaine Brée, introduction, in *Four Novels by Marguerite Duras* (New York: Grove Press, 1965), vi.

7. See Schuster, *Marguerite Duras Revisited*, 124–25.

8. Marguerite Duras, *Moderato cantabile*, trans. Richard Seaver, in *Four Novels by Marguerite Duras* (New York: Grove Press, 1965), 63; henceforth cited in the text.

9. From an interview of Duras by Susan D. Cohen quoted in Susan D. Cohen, *Women and Discourse in the Fiction of Marguerite Duras* (Amherst: University of Massachusetts Press, 1993), 9.

10. Duras and Gauthier, *Woman to Woman*, 37.

11. Leslie Hill, *Marguerite Duras: Apocalyptic Desires* (London: Routledge, 1993), 51.

12. Quoted in Schuster, *Marguerite Duras Revisited*, xxx.

13. Juliet Mitchell, introduction I, in Jacques Lacan, *Feminine Sexuality* (New York: W. W. Norton, 1982), 6.

14. See Carol J. Murphy, *Alienation and Absence in the Novels of Marguerite Duras* (Lexington, Kentucky: French Forum Publishers, 1982).

15. Marguerite Duras, *The Lover: A Novel*, trans. Barbara Bray (New York Pantheon, 1985), 37; henceforth cited in the text.

16. Schuster, *Marguerite Duras Revisited*, 116.

17. Ibid.

18. Marguerite Duras and Hervé Le Masson, "L'inconnue de la rue Catinat," *Le Nouvel Observateur* (28 September 1984): 52–54.

19. Jean Montalbetti, "Pacific Song," *Le Magazine Littéraire*, no. 211 (October 1984): 58.

20. Quoted in Cohen, *Women and Discourse in the Fiction of Marguerite Duras*, 89. My translation.

21. Schuster, *Marguerite Duras Revisited*, 123.

CHAPTER 8

1. Jean-François Lyotard, *The Postmodern Condition: A Report on Knowledge*, trans. Geoff Bennington and Brian Massumi (Minneapolis: University of Minnesota Press, 1979); Fredric Jameson, *Postmodernism, or, the Cultural Logic of Late Capitalism* (Durham: Duke University Press, 1991), 304.

2. A useful summary of the debate over this question is found in Ernst Behler, *Irony and the Discourse of Modernity* (Seattle: University of Washington Press, 1990), 3–36.

3. Morton P. Levitt, *Modernist Survivors: The Contemporary Novel in England, the United States, France, and Latin America* (Columbus: Ohio State University Press, 1987); *The Nouveau Roman Reader*, ed. John Fletcher and John Calder (London: John Calder, 1986).

4. Robbe-Grillet, *For a New Novel*, 10.

5. See Eric Gans, "The Last French Novels," *Romanic Review* 83,: 500–516.

6. Gérard Genette, *Narrative Discourse*, trans. Jane E. Lewis (Ithaca: Cornell University Press, 1980).

7. Anthony Trollope, *Barchester Towers* (London: Zodiac Press, 1962), 121–22. Quoted in Levitt, *Modernist Survivors*, 8.

8. Henry James, *The Art of Fiction*, quoted in Douwe W. Fokkema, *Literary History, Modernism, and Postmodernism* (Philadelphia: John Benjamins, 1984).

9. Levitt, *Modernist Survivors*, 8.

10. Jameson, *Postmodernism*, 1.

11. John Barth, *The Friday Book: Essays and Other Nonfiction* (New York: G. P. Putnam's Sons, 1984), 64.

12. Quoted in Barth, *The Friday Book*, 68–69.

13. Barth, *The Friday Book*, 69–70.

14. Quoted in Heath, *The Nouveau roman*, 69. My translation.

15. Behler, *Irony and the Discourse of Modernity*, 6.

16. Patricia Waugh, *Metafiction: The Theory and Practice of Self-Conscious Fiction* (London: Methuen, 1984).

17. Unless one takes the position that some postmodern attitude or mode of thinking turns up at various times in the past and is not confined to the postmodern age itself. If this is so, a new term should be coined, because the term "postmodern" is too dependent on a specific chronological period in the history of Western culture to be uprooted from that context and applied elsewhere.

18. Levitt, *Modernist Survivors*, 5.

19. On this aspect of Simon's work, see Jameson, *Postmodernism*, 131–53.

20. See Jameson, *Postmodernism*, xv.

Bibliography

This bibliography is highly selective in both primary and critical works. Further references may be found in the notes and in the secondary sources, listed below.

PRIMARY SOURCES

Novels and Essays by Michel Butor

6.810.000 Litres d'eau par seconde: étude stéréophonique. Paris: Gallimard, 1965. Translated as *Niagara: A Stereophonic Novel* by Elinor S. Miller (Chicago: Henry Regnery Co., 1969).

Degrés. Paris: Gallimard, 1960. Translated as *Degrees* by Richard Howard (New York: Simon and Schuster, 1962).

L'Emploi du temps. Paris: Les Editions de Minuit, 1956. Translated as *Passing Time* by Jean Stewart (New York: Simon and Schuster, 1960).

Improvisations sur Michel Butor: l'écriture en transformation. Paris: La Différence, 1993. Translated as *Improvisations on Butor: Transformation of Writing*, by Elinor S. Miller, edited by Lois Oppenheim (Gainesville: University Press of Florida, 1996).

Mobile, étude pour une représentation des Etats-Unis. Paris: Gallimard, 1962. Translated as *Mobile* by Richard Howard (New York: Simon and Schuster, 1963).

La Modification. Paris: Les Editions de Minuit, 1957. Translated as *A Change of Heart* by Jean Stewart (New York: Simon and Schuster, 1959).

Passage de Milan. Paris: Les Editions de Minuit, 1954.

Portrait de l'artiste en jeune singe: cappricio. Paris: Gallimard, 1967. Translated as *Portrait of the Artist as a Young Ape: A Caprice* by Dominic Di Bernardi (Normal, Ill.: Dalkey Archive Press, 1995).

Répertoire: Etudes et conférences 1948–1959. Paris: Les Editions de Minuit, 1960. Translated in part under the title *Inventory* and edited by Richard Howard (New York: Simon and Schuster, 1968). Includes essays from *Répertoire II*.

Répertoire II: études et conférences 1959–1963. Paris: Les Editions de Minuit, 1964. Translated in part as *Inventory* and edited by Richard Howard (New York: Simon and Schuster, 1968).

Répertoire III. Paris: Les Editions de Minuit, 1968.

Répertoire IV. Paris: Les Editions de Minuit, 1974.

Novels and Films by Marguerite Duras

L'Amant. Paris: Les Editions de Minuit, 1984. Translated as *The Lover* by Barbara Bray (New York: Pantheon Books, 1985).

L'Amant de la Chine du nord. Paris: Gallimard, 1991. Translated as *The North China Lover* by Leigh Hafrey (New York: The New Press, 1992).

L'Après-midi de M. Andesmas. Paris: Gallimard, 1962. Translated as *The After-
    noon of Mr. Andesmas* by Anne Borchardt in *Four Novels by Marguerite
    Duras*, introduction by Germaine Brée (New York: Grove Press, 1965).
Un Barrage contre le Pacifique. Paris: Gallimard, 1950. Translated as *The Sea
    Wall* by Herma Briffault (New York: Harper and Row, 1986).
Le Camion. Distributed by D. D. Productions, 1977. Film.
Détruire dit-elle. Distributed by S.N.A., 1969. Film.
Dix Heures et demie du soir en été. Paris: Gallimard, 1960. Translated as *10:30
    on a Summer Night* by Anne Borchardt in *Four Novels by Marguerite
    Duras*, introduction by Germaine Brée (New York: Grove Press, 1965).
Hiroshima mon amour. Paris: Gallimard, 1960. Translated as *Hiroshima mon
    amour* by Richard Seaver (New York: Grove Press, 1961). Film by Alain
    Renais (distributed by Zenith International Film Corp.), 1959.
India Song. Distributed by Films Armorial, 1974. Film.
Des Journées entières dans les arbres. Paris: Gallimard, 1954. Translated as
    Whole Days in the Trees by Anita Barrows (New York: Riverrun Press,
    1983).
Le Marin de Gibraltar. Paris: Gallimard, 1952. Translated as *The Sailor from
    Gibraltar* by Barbara Bray (New York: Grove Press, 1986).
Moderato cantabile. Paris: Les Editions de Minuit, 1958. Translated as *Moder-
    ato cantabile* by Richard Seaver in *Four Novels by Marguerite Duras*, intro-
    duction by Germaine Brée (New York: Grove Press, 1965).
Le Ravissement de Lol V. Stein. Paris: Gallimard, 1964. Translated as *The Rav-
    ishing of Lol Stein* by Richard Seaver (New York: Grove Press, 1966).
Le Square. Paris: Gallimard, 1954. Translated as *The Square* by Sonia Pitt-
    Rivers and Irina Murdoch in *Four Novels by Marguerite Duras*, introduc-
    tion by Germaine Brée (New York: Grove Press, 1965).
Le Vice-Consul. Paris: Gallimard, 1965. Translated as *The Vice-Consul* by
    Eileen Ellenbogen (New York: Pantheon, 1987).

                    Novels, Essays, and Films by Alain Robbe-Grillet

Angélique ou l'enchantement. Paris: Les Editions de Minuit, 1987.
L'année dernière à Marienbad. Paris: Les Editions de Minuit, 1961. Translated
    as *Last Year at Marienbad* by Richard Howard (New York: Grove Press,
    1962).
Dans le labyrinthe. Paris: Les Editions de Minuit, 1959. Translated as *In the
    Labyrinth* by Richard Howard (New York: Grove Press, 1960).
Djinn: un trou rouge entre les pavés disjoints. Paris: Les Editions de Minuit,
    1981. Translated as *Djinn* by Yvone Lenard and Walter Wells in *La Mai-
    son de Rendez-vous and Djinn* (New York: Grove Press, 1987).
Les Gommes. Paris: Les Editions de Minuit, 1953. Translated as *The Erasers* by
    Richard Howard (New York: Grove Press, 1964).
Instantanés. Paris: Les Editions de Minuit, 1962. Translated as *Snapshots: Sto-
    ries by Alain Robbe-Grillet* by Bruce Morrissette (New York: Grove Press,
    1968).
La Jalousie. Paris: Les Editions de Minuit, 1957. Translated as *Jealousy* by
    Richard Howard (New York: Grove Press, 1959).

La Maison de rendez-vous. Paris: Les Editions de Minuit, 1965. Translated as *La Maison de Rendez-vous* by Richard Howard (New York: Grove Press, 1966).

Le Miroir qui revient. Paris: Les Editions de Minuit, 1984. Translated as *Ghosts in the Mirror* by Jo Levy (New York: Grove Weidenfeld, 1991).

Pour un nouveau roman. Paris: Les Editions de Minuit, 1963. Translated as *For a New Novel: Essays on Fiction* by Richard Howard (New York: Grove Press, 1965).

Projet pour une révolution à New York. Paris: Les Editions de Minuit, 1970. Translated as *Project for a Revolution in New York* by Richard Howard (New York: Grove Press, 1972).

Un Régicide. Paris: Les Editions de Minuit, 1978. Robbe-Grillet's first novel, completed in 1949 but not published until 1978.

Souvenirs du triangle d'or. Paris: Les Editions de Minuit, 1978. Translated as *Recollections of the Golden Triangle* by J. A. Underwood (London: J. Calder, 1984).

Topologie d'une cité fantôme. Paris: Les Editions de Minuit, 1976. Translated as *Topology of a Phantom City* by J. A. Underwood (New York: Grove Press, 1977).

Trans-Europ-Express, 1966. Film.

Le Voyeur. Paris: Les Editions de Minuit, 1955. Translated as *The Voyeur* by Richard Howard (New York: Grove Press, 1958).

Novels and Essays by Nathalie Sarraute

"disent les imbéciles." Paris: Gallimard, 1976. Translated as *"fools say"* by Maria Jolas (New York: George Braziller, 1973).

Enfance. Paris: Gallimard, 1983. Translated as *Childhood: an autobiography* by Barbara Wright (New York: George Braziller, 1984).

Entre la Vie et la mort. Paris: Gallimard, 1968. Translated as *Between Life and Death* by Maria Jolas (New York: George Braziller, 1969).

L'Ere du soupçon. Paris: Gallimard, 1956. Translated as *The Age of Suspicion* by Maria Jolas (New York: George Braziller, 1963).

Les Fruits d'or. Paris: Gallimard, 1963. Translated as *The Golden Fruits* by Maria Jolas (New York: George Braziller, 1963).

Martereau. Paris: Gallimard, 1953. Translated as *Martereau* by Maria Jolas (New York: George Braziller, 1959).

Le Planétarium. Paris: Gallimard, 1959. Translated as *The Planetarium* by Maria Jolas (New York: George Braziller, 1960).

Portrait d'un inconnu. Paris: Robert Marin, 1948. Translated as *Portrait of a Man Unknown* by Maria Jolas (New York: George Braziller, 1958).

Tropismes. Paris: Robert Denoël, 1939. Translated as *Tropisms* by Maria Jolas (New York: George Braziller, 1963).

Tu ne t'aimes pas. Paris: Gallimard, 1989. Translated as *You don't love yourself: a novel* by Barbara Wright (New York: George Braziller, 1990).

L'Usage de la parole. Paris: Gallimard, 1980. Translated as *The use of speech* by Barbara Wright (New York: George Braziller, 1983).

Vous les entendez? Paris: Gallimard, 1970. Translated as *Do you hear them?* by Maria Jolas (New York: George Braziller, 1973).

Novels by Claude Simon

L'Acacia. Paris: Les Editions de Minuit, 1989. Translated as *The Acacia* by Richard Howard (New York: Pantheon, 1991).

La Bataille de Pharsale. Paris: Les Editions de Minuit, 1969. Translated as *The Battle of Pharsalus* by Richard Howard (New York: George Braziller, 1971).

Les Corps conducteurs. Paris: Les Editions de Minuit, 1971. Translated as *Conducting Bodies* by Helen R. Lane (New York: Grove Press, 1987).

Les Georgiques. Paris: Les Editions de Minuit, 1981. Translated as *The Georgics* by Beryl Fletcher and John Fletcher (London: John Calder, 1989).

L'Herbe. Paris: Les Editions de Minuit, 1958. Translated as *The Grass* by Richard Howard (New York: George Braziller, 1960).

Histoire. Paris: Les Editions de Minuit, 1967. Translated as *Histoire* by Richard Howard (New York: George Braziller, 1968).

L'Invitation. Paris: Les Editions de Minuit, 1987. Translated as *The Invitation* by Jim Cross (Elmwood Park, Ill.: Dalkey Archive Press, 1991).

Leçon de choses. Paris: Les Editions de Minuit, 1976. Translated as *The World About Us* by Daniel Weissbort (Princeton: Ontario Review Press, 1983).

Le Palace. Paris: Les Editions de Minuit, 1962. Translated as *The Palace* by Richard Howard (London: John Calder, 1963).

La Route des Flandres. Paris: Les Editions de Minuit, 1960. Translated as *The Flanders Road* by Richard Howard (London: John Calder, 1985).

Triptyque. Paris: Les Editions de Minuit, 1973. Translated as *Triptych* by Helen R. Lane (New York: Viking, 1976).

Le Vent: Tentative de restitution d'un retable baroque. Paris: Les Editions de Minuit, 1957. Translated as *The Wind* by Richard Howard (New York: George Braziller, 1959).

SECONDARY SOURCES

Barthes, Roland. *Critical Essays*, translated by Richard Howard. Evanston: Northwestern University Press, 1972. Includes three influential early articles about Robbe-Grillet.

Barth, John. *The Friday Book: Essays and Other Nonfiction*. New York: G. P. Putnam's Sons, 1984. Postmodernist thinking about fiction from an American novelist.

Behler, Ernst. *Irony and the Discourse of Modernity*. Seattle: University of Washington Press, 1990. A useful introduction to modern and postmodern theories.

Bell, Sheila M. *Nathalie Sarraute: "Portrait d'un inconnu" and "Vous les entendez?"* London: Grant & Cutler, Critical Guides to French Texts, 1988. A valuable discussion of two of Sarraute's novels.

Bernal, Olga. *Alain Robbe-Grillet: le roman de l'absence*. Paris: Gallimard, 1964. A phenomenological approach to Robbe-Grillet's early novels.

Besser, Gretchen Rous. *Nathalie Sarraute*. Boston: Twayne, 1979. A useful introduction to Sarraute.

Brewer, Maria Minich. *Claude Simon: Narrativities without Narrative*. Lincoln: University of Nebraska Press, 1995. Approaches Simon's work from the standpoint of his complex attitude toward narrative order.

Britton, Celia. *Claude Simon: Writing the Visible*. Cambridge: Cambridge University Press, 1987. Includes an interesting evaluation of recent criticism of Simon.

———. *The Nouveau Roman: Fiction, Theory, Politics*. New York: St. Martin's, Press, 1992.

Carroll, David. *The Subject in Question: The Languages of Theory and the Strategies of Fiction*. Chicago: University of Chicago Press, 1982. An important application of modern critical theory to the works of Claude Simon.

Culler, Jonathan. *Roland Barthes*. New York: Oxford University Press, 1983. Interesting discussion of Robbe-Grillet's role in Barthes's early thought, as well as a valuable discussion of the whole of Barthes's work.

Dällenbach, Lucien. *Claude Simon*. Paris: Editions du Seuil, 1988. Lucid view of Simon's works by a highly influential critic.

Duffy, Jean H. *Butor: "La Modification."* London: Grant & Cutler, 1990. A useful guide to Butor's novel, with emphasis on phenomenological issues.

Duncan, Alastair. *Claude Simon: Adventures in Words*. Manchester: Manchester University Press, 1994. A valuable introduction to Simon's works, with very useful information on the critical context of the New Novel.

Fletcher, John, and John Calder, eds. *The Nouveau Roman Reader*. London: John Calder, 1986. Excerpts from New Novel texts, with a substantial introduction.

Fokkema, Douwe W. *Literary History, Modernism, and Postmodernism*. Philadelphia: John Benjamins, 1984. A clear and concise discussion of modernist and postmodernist tendencies in literature.

Heath, Stephen. *The Nouveau roman: A Study in the Practice of Writing*. Philadelphia: Temple University Press, 1972. An excellent study, with emphasis on the second-phase conception of the New Novel.

Hofmann, Carol. *Forgetting and Marguerite Duras*. Niwot, Col.: University Press of Colorado, 1991. An interesting study of the themes of repression, repetition, and mourning in Duras.

Hollier, Denis, ed. *A New History of French Literature*. Cambridge: Harvard University Press, 1989. An authoritative, up-to-date guide to French literature in its cultural context.

Jameson, Fredric. *Postmodernism, or, The Cultural Logic of Late Capitalism*. Durham: Duke University Press, 1991. An essential work on postmodernism. Chapter 5, "Reading and the Division of Labor," is about Claude Simon.

Jefferson, Ann. *The Nouveau Roman and the Poetics of Fiction*. Cambridge: Cambridge University Press, 1980.

Leki, Ilona. *Alain Robbe-Grillet*. Boston: Twayne Publishers, 1983. A valuable introduction to Robbe-Grillet's work.

Levitt, Morton P. *Modernist Survivors*. Columbus: Ohio State University Press, 1987. A view of the New Novelists as modernists.

Loubère, J.A.E. *The Novels of Claude Simon*. Ithaca: Cornell University Press, 1975. An excellent introduction to Simon's work.

Mercier, Vivian. *The New Novel from Queneau to Pinget*. New York: Farrar, Strauss and Giroux, 1971. A useful and accessible survey of the field.

Morrissette, Bruce. *Intertextual Assemblages in Robbe-Grillet from Topology to the Golden Triangle*. Fredericton, New Brunswick: York Press, 1979. About Robbe-Grillet's later work.

———. *The Novels of Robbe-Grillet*. Ithaca: Cornell University Press, 1975. First published in French in 1963, this is a highly influential study.

Oppenheim, Lois, ed. *Three Decades of the French New Novel*. Urbana: University of Illinois Press, 1986. The proceedings of a 1982 colloquium in New York, with an excellent introduction.

Raillard, Georges, ed. *Butor: Colloque de Cerisy*. Paris: Union générale d'editions, 1974. Proceedings of the Cerisy colloquium on Butor's work.

Ramsay, Raylene. *Robbe-Grillet and Modernity: Science, Sexuality and Subversion*. Gainesville: University Press of Florida, 1992. Ramsay takes a very different approach to modernity than the one presented here.

Ricardou, Jean, ed. *Lire Claude Simon: Colloque de Cerisy*. Paris: Union générale d'éditions, 1975. Proceedings of the Cerisy colloquium on Simon's work.

———. *Problèmes du nouveau roman*. Paris: Editions du Seuil, 1967. Influential book by the critic most associated with the second phase of the New Novel.

———, ed. *Robbe-Grillet: Colloque de Cerisy*. 2 vols. Paris: Union générale d'éditions, 1976. Proceedings of the Cerisy colloquium on Robbe-Grillet's work.

Ricardou, Jean, and Françoise van Rossum-Guyon, eds. *Nouveau roman: hier, aujourd'hui*. 2 vols. Paris, Union générale d'éditions, 1972. Proceedings of the Cerisy colloquium on the New Novel.

Roudiez, Leon S. *French Fiction Today: A New Direction*. New Brunswick: Rutgers University Press, 1972. An interesting and useful overview of some 15 writers, not limited to New Novelists.

Schuster, Marilyn R. *Marguerite Duras Revisited*. New York: Twayne Publishers, 1993. An excellent introduction to Duras, with a very useful overview of recent work on the author.

Spencer, Michael. *Michel Butor*. New York: Twayne Publishers, 1974. Thorough and original readings of Butor's works.

Sturrock, John. *The French New Novel: Claude Simon, Michel Butor, Alain Robbe-Grillet*. London: Oxford University Press, 1969. An excellent overview of the subject.

Index

The Author

Arthur Babcock is associate professor of French at the University of Southern California. He received B.A., M.A., and Ph.D. degrees at the University of Michigan. He is the author of *Portraits of Artists: Reflexivity in Gidean Fiction, 1902–1946* (York, South Carolina: French Literature Publications Co., 1982) and of articles on French and European literature of the nineteenth and twentieth centuries and foreign-language pedagogy.

The Editor

Herbert Sussman, professor of English at Northeastern University, is the author of *Victorian Masculinities: Method and Masculine Poetics in Early Victorian Literature and Art; Fact into Figure: Typology in Carlyle, Ruskin, and the Pre-Raphaelite Brotherhood;* and *Victorians and the Machine: The Literary Response to Technology.*